cooking made simple

Alexandra Dudley

Foolproof recipes for busy people

EBURY
PRESS

TOSSED 10

FRIED 42

STIRRED 66

BAKED 90

GRILLED 128

SUGARED 152

BETTER BASICS 182

INTRODUCTION

Cooking, and cooking well, does not need to be difficult. The truth is that a good meal – an excellent meal even – does not have to equate to endless hours in the kitchen, nor does it always demand patience. I am not a complicated cook, but I am a good cook. I have cooked in tiny kitchens and I have cooked in vast kitchens. I have cooked for two and I have cooked for 20. There are recipes that require the utmost precision and hours of dedication – but you will not find them in this book. Instead, you'll find dishes that look as though they required three varying ways of cooking but are, in fact, the joyful result of everything thrown into one tray. You will find sides and salads that take 10 minutes to prepare, but piled high onto a platter will happily eclipse the rest of the dinner table. These are the recipes I've emailed to friends who are in a panic about cooking for a lover for the first time, the recipes I've WhatsApp'd to my brother midweek when he says he's bored of everything in his fridge but wants something delicious on the table in 15 minutes. They are the recipes I've sent to the friends who claim that they 'can't cook' along with the simple note of 'you can'. Many of them have found their way back to me, pinged over in smudgy candlelit images through friends-of-friends who've found themselves eating them at a dinner party, or on the sofa with their mum. These are the recipes that I have cooked successfully time and time again, for my husband, for friends, or even just for me.

Simple is a word that can mean different things to different people, particularly in the kitchen. What might sound simple to a practiced cook, can seem very daunting to someone else with less confidence. However, years of cooking has taught me that many of the things I perhaps once deemed as complicated, are in fact not. Baking your own bread may sound tedious until you've made a loaf of soda bread and seen just how simple it can be. You may look at a squidgy focaccia and assume that only hours of kneading could have produced those bubbles, when in fact most of the magic happens as the dough has a 12-hour chill in the fridge, leaving you free to get a good night's sleep. Whipped feta, labneh, gnudi or sage and pecan browned butter may all sound rather impressive, but the truth is most of them involve two simple steps. I've tried to fill this book with recipes that look great and taste even better, and that anyone can cook, no matter their level of experience. If you come across recipes that seem intimidating, I encourage you to read on and cook on. You'll be left with something delicious to eat, and the even better feeling of 'I made that!'.

Like most people who live in a city, I have a very small kitchen. My cupboards are a Tetris-puzzle of ceramics and glassware I've collected over the years, with rubber-banded packets of flour and repurposed peanut butter jars of seeds and spices shoved-in wherever they can fit. My kitchen is not one of those minimal serene spaces you see on the back pages of glossy magazines with pristine sandstone countertops and everything tucked away. It's busy and full, with drawers bursting with wooden spoons and too many corkscrews, and recipes sellotaped to the inside of cupboards. My saucepans and oven trays are a game of Jenga that only I know how to play, and the surrounding area by the sink is so small that there's really only room for one person. Despite all this, I cook a lot. I cook every day, sometimes for many. The secret to this, and the reason I wrote this book, is not to overcrowd any one part of my kitchen. It's no use serving five dishes that all require a hob when you only have four rings. Better to have two salads that you can prep ahead and something that can bubble happily on the hob for a while, or perhaps just one dish that simply needs to be flung into the oven half an hour before sitting down.

So I've chosen to divide the recipes in this book into seven parts, separating them into where you'll make them in the kitchen: Tossed: the recipes you can throw together on your kitchen counter. Fried: the ones you cook (usually quickly) in a frying pan. Stirred: the ones that bubble on the hob. Baked and Grilled: which make the most of your oven timings and settings or, weather permitting,

the BBQ. There is also, of course, Sugared, a chapter dedicated to sweet things, all of which can either be prepped well ahead or come together with little notice – because no meal is complete without pudding. Then lastly, you'll also find a chapter of Better Basics. These are things that are often the key component in taking something from good to great. They are the recipes that I rely on and return to when something needs a little oomph or perhaps that little bit extra to make it complete. All of them can be tuned and paired with a variety of accompaniments and bring with them texture, flavour or substance that inevitably makes the end result better.

My hope is that this book will encourage you to cook when you don't really feel like cooking, that it will make quick mid-week suppers something to look forward to (without resulting in piles of washing up), and give you the confidence to cook something you might have once dismissed as complicated. I want to teach you how best to navigate your kitchen (however small it is), how to prep, how to plan and how to make it all work out, even when there's no time for prepping or planning at all.

ON PLANNING

Thinking of what to cook for supper every night can be exhausting, especially when we are busy. I try to have an idea of what I'll cook for perhaps three nights of the week. It guarantees that I'll be eating something good most of the time, and usually I'll cook more than I need. I am a big fan of cooking once and eating twice and a bit of forward planning means there's freedom for more creativity outside of the plan, too. Often my most enjoyable meals have come about from a combination of leftovers and what's knocking about in the fridge. I've also included tips for getting ahead, so that you can get any prep done ahead of time and throw things together at the last minute.

TIME

Sometimes there is lots of time to spend in the kitchen and sometimes there is none at all. I love the days when I can spend a leisurely day making pasta or an extravagant pudding before sitting down to a big feast, but more often than not I'm juggling bath time, emails and three lots of washing all while cooking dinner. I love the ease of a one-tray, or something that needs a quick chop and a simmer and can sit happily for a couple of hours. I've learnt not to overstretch myself, whether I'm cooking just for me or for friends. I've indicated how long the recipes take in this book so that you can choose something that suits you at a quick glance. I've suggested recipes that work with each other, too, to help you pair things together, but do not feel bound by this, Remember you are the boss of your own kitchen.

SPACE

My kitchen at home is not vast and I have had to learn how best to utilise the space when cooking, especially when cooking for many. I chose to divide the chapters into where you make recipes in the kitchen because I have found this the most comfortable and enjoyable way to cook. It could be that the potatoes mainly need the hob and just a few chives stirred through before serving, which means the oven is free for something, be it fish, chicken or some good veg. Then there's probably a sizeable area of countertop to toss together a salad or assemble something a bit more fiddly to snack on. I like to divide my countertop into different sections, too. A Mise-en-place is a fancy French restaurant term for 'putting things in place' or having everything ready. But it's also a practise that is useful in home cooking and something I find especially useful when working with a small space. Things like mixing dressings, plucking herbs or chopping garlic and onions for the base of a dish can all be done ahead, and again, I've included 'do aheads' so that you can easily see what can be done in advance, making the cooking process smoother and quicker, and without a tower of dishes piling up in the sink.

BALANCE

A good meal ticks the box but a great meal ticks all of them. Where something is warm either in flavour or heat, it will usually be bettered by the addition of something cool or acidic. It could be as simple as a spoonful of crème fraîche or a squeeze of lemon to finish things off, but it is a useful rule to lean on when cooking especially when seasoning. If something feels a bit lacking in spark or flavour, think opposites, as it's likely that will spring the dish into life. Sweeter vegetables like carrots or red peppers will sing with a splash of vinegar. A handful of crunchy seeds can transform a leafy salad from the sidelines to star of the table. The same rule can be applied when pairing dishes. If you're serving something creamy and rich, think about complementing it with something crunchy and fresh. The recipe pairing suggestions on each recipe take this into account, and I've suggested some menu scenarios at the end of the book to serve as inspiration, too.

PLATING

Some dishes lend themselves to being plated individually, but for the most part, I am a fan of serving things sharing-style. It tends to mean there's less faff in the kitchen and that things will stay warmer for longer during the journey from kitchen to table, too. I like to think about different shapes when choosing serving dishes but chiefly about height! I prefer salads piled onto platters rather than sinking into bowls (they also tend to stay crisper for longer this way). I like to choose dishes that are slightly smaller than one might deem ideal. It makes the food look more plentiful and also means there's more space to fit everything on the table. I have two cake stands that rarely act as the base for cakes, and they are more often used as a platform for toasted soldiers of focaccia or to propel piles of hot buttery flatbreads closer to wandering hands, while bottles open and glasses clink. There should always be salt on the table (no matter how brilliant you think your nose for seasoning is). A handful of fresh herbs is a simple way to bring a bit of oomph to pretty much anything, and almost everything can be improved by a final drizzle of good olive oil or a squeeze of lemon.

COOKING FOR MORE THAN JUST FAMILY

I love to host, and a lot of the recipes in this book can be doubled and tripled easily if you find yourself with more than two or four people to cook for. Entertaining can feel daunting, but if you let go of the idea that everything must be impressive, perfect and finished before your guests arrive, it doesn't have to be stressful at all. I've never been averse to cutting corners, and if there are routes to simplify things without compromising on taste, I will always take them. If you come to my house, it's not uncommon for me to find a job for you to do. For years I did everything myself, guests poking their head in with an 'is there anything I can do?', while I practically fell over the oven door to say that 'no, there was really nothing at all' and insisted they go and enjoy their spritzer! All the while semi-envious of the party fizzing along, while I frantically prepared bruschetta. Until one day I tried something new. I plonked the whole thing on the edge of the table for everyone to get involved. The thing is, people often really do want to do something to help. Preparing food together can be as delightful as eating it together. At the very least, it is a conversation starter. So my advice when it comes to cooking for others is not to be a host with the most, but to be a host that shares. Perhaps someone can pour the wine while another slices bread, and another watches that it doesn't burn on the grill. Someone can rub the charred bread with garlic, and perhaps you can spoon over the tomatoes. It may be a far cry from the restaurant experience, but isn't that one of the best things about just cooking at home? That it's personal, intimate and perfectly imperfect.

TOSSED

ASPARAGUS AND GREEN BEAN MIMOSA SALAD
15

ARTICHOKE, FENNEL AND PARMESAN SALAD
16

HERB SALAD WITH CRUSHED HAZELNUTS
18

NECTARINES WITH BURRATA AND PINK PEPPERCORNS
20

QUEEN CAESAR SALAD
23

CARROT AND CORIANDER SALAD
24

SALSA VERDE SALAD
25

LOADED FETA WITH PEACH, OLIVES AND HERBS
28

SMOKY CHIPOTLE PRAWN COCKTAIL
30

CHICORY AND PEAR SEEDED SALAD
32

GREEN BEANS WITH BASIL AND PINE NUTS
34

WINTER GREENS WITH ALMONDS AND FIGS
37

BITTER LEAF SALAD WITH SOFT EGGS
38

ZA'ATAR CABBAGE, FENNEL, APPLE SLAW
40

TOMATO SALAD
41

Despite cooking often, I am neither the most organised person, nor the most patient. Most of my favourite recipes are those that come together quickly. Fresh ingredients thrown together with a good dressing and perhaps a handful of crunchy breadcrumbs or crushed hazelnuts. Tossed, is the chapter dedicated to this sort of cooking. These are recipes that uplift any occasion and have been enjoyed at my table time and time again. They are the ones I will pile high onto platters alongside torn chunks of bread when we decide, last minute, to have ten over for supper, and the recipes I lean on most when the weeknight omelette needs a bit of a chorus. I toyed with the idea of calling this chapter 'salads' but I felt that it didn't do the recipes justice. These are salads with oomph. They are crunchy, zesty and textured. The ones that always demand second helpings and that work very well just as they are, or make excellent accompaniments to the dishes that are a little richer and need the balancing act of something fresh. They are moreish and delicious, and usually the ones that go first, but best of all, they are simple and can be tossed together with very little time.

Asparagus and green bean mimosa salad

I love this salad. Crunchy and satisfying, it is one that I often make for lunch. The eggs are pleasingly filling, while perky blanched greens and toasted pine nuts deliver on crunch. All you need is a fork and perhaps a wedge of good bread to mop up the last of the dressing. The classic mimosa salad is something you'll often see on a French menu, and is traditionally made with hard-boiled eggs that are then usually finely grated or traditionally pushed through a sieve. I prefer my eggs on the jammy side and so keep them halved or quartered. I love the addition of green beans for a bit more bite and often make it with green beans alone when asparagus is not in season. Tarragon is wonderful here, but feel free to switch things up with parsley, chives or dill. Toasted almonds, walnuts or sunflower seeds are lovely in the place of pine nuts, too.

Serves 4
Time 20 minutes

30g pine nuts
4 large eggs, at room temperature
2 bunches of asparagus
300g green beans
2 tbsp capers, rinsed and drained
Small bunch of tarragon (about 20g), leaves roughly chopped (about 2 tbsp)

For the dressing

1 heaped tsp Dijon mustard
2 tbsp red wine vinegar or sherry vinegar
Olive oil

Toast the pine nuts first by cooking them in a dry frying pan over a gentle heat until golden brown. Allow to cool.

Bring a pan of water to the boil. Lower in the eggs and boil for 7 minutes. After 7 minutes, scoop the eggs out of the pan and immediately plunge them into a bowl of ice-cold water. Let them cool for 5 minutes.

Meanwhile, trim away any woody ends from the asparagus and pinch off the top stalks from the beans. Bring a pan of salted water to the boil, then blanch the asparagus with the green beans for 2–3 minutes. Drain the vegetables while they are still crisp, then plunge them into ice-cold water to stop them cooking further. Drain again and pat dry with a clean tea towel.

In a large bowl, whisk together the mustard and vinegar along with enough olive oil to create a glossy, emulsified dressing.

Using the flat of your knife, run the blade over the capers to roughly smoosh them. Add the capers and the chopped tarragon to the dressing bowl.

Toss the asparagus and beans into the bowl, then add the toasted pine nuts. Transfer everything to a serving plate.

When cool enough to handle, peel the boiled eggs. Halve or quarter the eggs and arrange them over the salad. Finish with more chopped tarragon, if you like.

Do aheads

- Every ingredient in this salad benefits from being cool, so you can blanch the asparagus and beans ahead of time and keep in the fridge. Toss everything with the dressing just before serving.
- The dressing can be made ahead of time – there is no need to refrigerate it.

Goes well with

- Pan-fried chicken with chilli, tomatoes and mint **p. 58**
- Artichoke, fennel and parmesan salad **p. 16**
- Wholegrain focaccia **p. 202**

Artichoke, fennel and parmesan salad

I make it a habit to always have a jar of marinated artichokes in the cupboard. They make even the simplest of suppers feel more luxurious. Here, they are combined with crunchy raw fennel, capers, parsley, Parmesan and lots of lemon to create a light yet satisfying salad. This can almost double up as a good condiment, too, especially when paired with chicken or fish.

Serves 4
Time 10 minutes

- 2 fennel bulbs, trimmed
- Juice of 1 lemon
- 150g jarred marinated artichokes, drained
- 2 tbsp capers, rinsed and drained
- 40g Grana Padano or Parmesan
- Handful of parsley leaves
- Olive oil

Finely slice the fennel using a sharp knife or mandolin. Place into a large bowl and toss in the lemon juice to stop it going brown.

Slice the artichokes into roughly 5mm slices or wedges and smoosh the capers by running the flat of your knife over them a few times on the chopping board. Add both to the bowl with the fennel.

Using a vegetable peeler, shave thin slices of the Grana Padano or Parmesan. Feel free to be generous here. More is more.

Add the parsley leaves, a generous slosh of olive oil and a pinch of salt and toss everything together. Taste to check the seasoning, adjusting with more lemon juice, olive oil or salt as necessary.

Goes well with
- Salsa verde salad **p. 25**
- Chicken with saffron and chickpeas **p. 104**
- Baked chicken with La Ratte potatoes and romesco **p. 111**

Herb salad with crushed hazelnuts

Brimming with fresh herbs, this salad is reminiscent of tabbouleh; however, rather than bulgur wheat, it is generously filled with roasted hazelnuts in place of the grains. The plucking of the herbs is somewhat a labour of love, but one that is worth it. This salad works very well alongside some grilled or barbecued fish, or even as a bit of an outfit for a blob of creamy burrata. I love it with some crispy potatoes or rösti (see page 62).

Serves 4
Time 15 minutes

100g blanched hazelnuts
Large bunch of tarragon (about 40g)
Large bunch of parsley (about 40g)
Small bunch of dill (about 20g)
Small bunch of mint (about 20g)
100g rocket leaves

For the dressing

1 tsp fennel seeds
1 tsp black mustard seeds
1 tsp caraway seeds
Grated zest of 1 unwaxed lemon
Juice of ½ lemon
1 tbsp runny honey
2 tbsp moscatel vinegar or red wine vinegar
4 tbsp olive oil
Coarse sea salt flakes

Preheat the oven to 180°C fan.

Arrange the hazelnuts in a single layer on a baking sheet and roast for 10 minutes or until they begin to turn golden and smell nutty. Allow to cool. Once cool, place the hazelnuts in a clean, dry tea towel and fold over. Using a rolling pin, roughly crush the nuts, then transfer to a small bowl and set aside.

Meanwhile, in a dry frying pan set over a medium heat, toast the fennel seeds, mustard seeds and caraway seeds for the dressing until they begin to pop and release their aromas. Transfer to a large bowl.

Add the grated zest from the lemon to the bowl with the toasted seeds, then squeeze in the juice from half of the lemon. Add the honey, vinegar, olive oil and a good pinch of sea salt flakes, then whisk to combine into a dressing.

Pluck the herbs from their stems and add to a bowl with the rocket, then add to the bowl with the dressing. Scatter in the crushed hazelnuts and toss everything together. Check and adjust the seasoning, adding more salt or lemon juice as necessary. Transfer to a serving plate.

Do aheads

- The seeds for the dressing can be toasted and the dressing can be made ahead of time – there is no need to refrigerate it.
- The hazelnuts can be roasted and crushed ahead of time.

Goes well with

- Potato rösti with fried eggs and soft herbs **p. 62**
- Baked salmon with blood orange and chilli **p. 122**
- Grilled sugar snap peas with lemony ricotta **p. 133**

Nectarines with burrata and pink peppercorns

Peppercorns might seem like an odd ingredient to pair with fruit, but believe me when I say they bring an entirely new level of flavour. Pink peppercorns are far less aggressive than black ones and have more of a sweet-sour peppiness to them, which goes brilliantly with sweet nectarines and zingy lime. I cook with them so often that I tend to purchase them in bulk from spice stalls or online, but they are now stocked in most supermarkets as well. If you have peaches rather than nectarines, they are also very good in this, as is mozzarella if you cannot get hold of burrata. This makes for a very delicious lunch piled onto a thick slice of toast, but it's also a very good starter or sharing side.

Serves 4
Time 10 minutes

2 ripe nectarines (or peaches)
150g ball of burrata (or mozzarella)
Grated zest of 1 lime, to garnish

For the dressing

3 tbsp olive oil
1 tbsp runny honey
2 red bird's eye chillies, deseeded and finely chopped
Juice of ½ lime
1½ tsp pink peppercorns, crushed (plus extra to garnish)
Pinch of salt (plus extra to garnish)

Combine all the ingredients for the dressing in a small bowl.

Cut each nectarine in half and remove the stone. Roughly chop or tear the fruit and add to a serving plate or bowl. Keeping some of the dressing back for the burrata, toss the fruit in most of the dressing.

Arrange the burrata in the centre of the plate or bowl and spoon over the remaining dressing. Sprinkle over some more crushed pink peppercorns and salt, then finish with the lime zest.

Do aheads

The dressing can be made ahead of time – there is no need to refrigerate it.

Goes well with

- Carrot and coriander salad **p. 24**
- Fruit and nut rice **p. 87**
- Grilled aubergines with green tahini **p. 134**

Queen Caesar salad

I call this a Queen Caesar Salad because it looks so wonderfully regal on the table, but it is really a simple Caesar salad dressed up in a way to make it a little more 'wow'. I make my Caesar dressing with yogurt, which makes for a slightly lighter yet still creamy dressing. The anchovy-chilli breadcrumbs have a good kick of heat, which I think really makes this, but if you are sensitive to heat, either reduce or omit the chilli. I usually make my own breadcrumbs by whizzing up some stale or toasted bread in a food processor but you can use storebought. I recommend washing the lettuce ahead of preparing the salad, so that it has enough time to drain.

Serves 4
Time 15 minutes

1 large butterhead lettuce (or 4 baby gem lettuces)

For the breadcrumbs

Olive oil

5 tinned anchovies, roughly chopped (keep the rest to garnish)

½ tsp chilli flakes (or use ¼ tsp if sensitive to heat)

40g breadcrumbs

For the dressing

150g thick Greek yogurt

30g tin of anchovies in oil, drained

1 small garlic clove, peeled

1 tsp Dijon mustard

Juice of ½ lemon

1 tbsp olive oil

Good handful of Grana Padano or Parmesan (about 30g), finely grated (plus extra to garnish)

Carefully trim the base of the lettuce so that it has a flat bottom, then carefully wash it. I do this by giving it a good swim in a large bowl filled with cold water and turning it upside down on my drying rack to drain. A colander would work too, although a large salad spinner would be more efficient.

Next, prepare the breadcrumbs. Heat a good glug of olive oil in a frying pan over a medium heat. Add the anchovies to the pan and cook until melted down. Add the chilli flakes and breadcrumbs and cook until golden, stirring often. Transfer to a plate lined with kitchen paper to drain any excess oil.

Put all the ingredients for the dressing in a high-speed blender (such as a Nutribullet) and blitz until smooth and creamy.

Sit the washed lettuce on a large serving plate and drizzle over most of the dressing, making sure it cascades between all the folds of the leaves. Scatter the breadcrumbs over the lettuce, then evenly layer on the remaining whole anchovies. Finely grate over more Grana Padano or Parmesan using a Microplane grater to finish.

Slice the lettuce into big wedges, as you would a cake, and load slices onto everyone's plates. Transfer any remaining dressing to a small jug and place on the table for people to add more, if they like.

Do aheads

- I like to wash the lettuce an hour or so before preparing the salad so it has time to drain.
- The dressing can be made up to a day ahead but keep it refrigerated until serving.
- The breadcrumbs can be made a day ahead.

Goes well with

- One-tray spatchcocked chicken with herby rice **p. 114**
- New potatoes with anchovy chive butter **p. 77**
- Pea, pancetta and pecorino tart **p. 100**

Carrot and coriander salad

Carrot and coriander are a classic pairing and the key players in one of my favourite soups. The idea for this salad came from finding myself with almost a kilo of carrots and a rather sad-looking bunch of coriander after clearing out the fridge. The finished dish was so delicious that it has become a bit of a staple. It is more of a slaw than a salad but one that works well with warm dishes, too.

Serves 4–6
Time 20 minutes

50g sunflower seeds
2 tsp coriander seeds
4 tbsp olive oil
2 tbsp sherry vinegar
1 tbsp runny honey
750g carrots, peeled
Small bunch of coriander (about 25g)

In a dry frying pan set over a low heat, toast the sunflower seeds for 5–6 minutes or until they begin to turn golden and smell nutty. Transfer to a plate to cool.

In the same pan, toast the coriander seeds over a low heat for 3 minutes or until they begin to smell fragrant. Transfer to a pestle and mortar and gently crush. (You can also use a small bowl and the base of a spice jar or end of a rolling pin for this.)

In a large bowl, combine the olive oil, sherry vinegar, honey and crushed coriander seeds.

Using the large holes of a box grater, coarsely grate the carrots into the bowl.

Finely chop the coriander and add to the bowl. There is no need to separate the leaves from the stems, just roughly tear the bunch before chopping it.

Add the toasted sunflower seeds to the bowl with the carrots and coriander, then toss everything in the dressing just before serving.

Do aheads
- The sunflower seeds can be toasted up to 7 days ahead and kept in a sealed jar.
- The dressing can be made up to 3 days ahead and kept in a sealed container on the counter.

Goes well with
- Pan-fried seabass with olive salsa **p. 64**
- Harissa sesame carrots with labneh **p. 95**
- Chicken with saffron and chickpeas **p. 104**

Salsa verde salad

I could happily eat a bowl of salsa verde with a spoon. Made from a medley of herbs, capers, garlic and anchovies, it is a punchy, flavourful sauce usually enjoyed with grilled fish or meat and sometimes vegetables. This recipe came about as the result of a happy accident one lazy Saturday lunchtime when my husband and I were feeling a little worse for wear after being up all night with our newborn. We craved something fresh and crunchy. There was half a bowl of salsa verde in the fridge leftover from a roast chicken the night before; rather than mix up a salad dressing, I just tossed the lot in with the leaves along with a handful of leftover shredded chicken. It was exactly what we needed and is now a salad I make on repeat. *Pictured overleaf.*

Serves 4
Time 10 minutes

5 baby gem lettuces

For the salsa verde

Large bunch of parsley (about 100g), leaves torn

Medium bunch of mint (about 50g), leaves picked

Medium bunch of tarragon, basil or dill (about 50g)

2 tbsp capers, rinsed and drained

6 tinned anchovy fillets

1 large garlic clove, finely chopped or grated

1 heaped tsp Dijon mustard

2 tbsp red wine vinegar

Juice of ½ lemon (or more to taste)

Pinch of salt

6 tbsp olive oil

Place all the ingredients for the salsa verde in a high-speed blender (such as a Nutribullet) and blitz to combine. You may need to pulse a few times to get it going. If it is resisting, add a little more olive oil. Check the seasoning, adding more lemon juice to taste, if necessary. It should be sharp and vibrant.

Separate the leaves from the baby gem, then gently wash and drain them. Toss the lettuce leaves in a bowl with the salsa verde until well coated. Transfer to a serving bowl if you wish.

Do aheads

The salsa verde can be made up to 3 days ahead and stored in the fridge.

Goes well with
- Pan-fried chicken with chilli, tomatoes and mint (also pictured overleaf) **p. 58**
- Baked ricotta with romano peppers **p. 102**
- Baked chicken with La Ratte potatoes and romesco **p. 111**

Loaded feta with peach, olives and herbs

Whenever I am lucky enough to visit Greece, I always return home with an amplified love for feta and stone fruit. Cycling to the local grocer and picking out the perfect peach before heading to the beach has become something of a holiday ritual. A crucial step to the best peach on the beach is to wash it in the sea. The saltiness of the sea water is divine against the sweet flesh of the fruit. It is the summers of salty, sea-washed peaches that inspired this salad, which is perfect when you fancy something flavourful but simple to prepare. Here, I serve the salad piled over a whole block of feta which can then be broken at the table, making it a great sharing dish for everyone to get their forks into.

Serves 4
Time 15 minutes

1 tsp coriander seeds
Large handful of rocket leaves
Large handful of mint leaves
Large handful of parsley leaves
40g Kalamata olives
1 tbsp capers, rinsed and drained
3 tbsp olive oil
1 tbsp moscatel vinegar or sherry vinegar
1 ripe peach (or nectarine)
150–200g block of feta

In a dry frying pan set over a low heat, toast the coriander seeds for 3–4 minutes or until they begin to smell fragrant. Transfer to a pestle and mortar and gently crush. (You can also use a small bowl and the base of a spice jar or end of a rolling pin for this.)

Wash and drain the rocket and herbs, then pluck the leaves from the herbs (there is no need to chop them). Place everything in a bowl.

Tear the Kalamata olives, squeezing out the stones as you do so, and drop them into the bowl. Add the capers and crushed coriander seeds to the salad. Drizzle in the olive oil and vinegar, then add a good pinch of salt. Gently toss to coat all the ingredients.

Cut the peach in half and remove the stone. Slice the fruit into segments, add them to the salad and gently toss again.

Place the block of feta on a serving plate. Pile the rocket and peach salad on top of the cheese to cover it. Break the feta into pieces at the table, tossing everything together just before serving.

Do aheads

This salad can be made at very short notice, but you can toast the coriander seeds ahead of time.

Goes well with

- Chicken with saffron and chickpeas p. 104
- Harissa honey chicken wings p. 151
- Wholegrain flatbreads p. 199
- Grilled aubergines with green tahini p. 134

Smoky chipotle prawn cocktail

One of the first cookbooks I remember looking at as a child was my mother's copy of *The Prawn Cocktail Years* by Lindsey Bareham and Simon Hopkinson. It is filled with recipes that, at the time of its publication, were already considered retro: Black Forest Gâteau, Crêpes Suzette and Coq au Vin. The front cover is almost entirely filled by a glossy photograph of a prawn cocktail. A fat wedge of lemon sticks out at the top, while a plump pink prawn dangles over the side, its pink whiskers curling around the base of the silver coupe. I thought it was the most glorious, brilliant thing I had ever seen. The classic prawn cocktail will be forever fabulous, but I do love this more relaxed way of serving it. It is easier to prepare and works well for a quick lunch, too. The smoky chipotle chilli adds a rich warmth as well as a spicy kick, and it is delicious with juicy chilled prawns.

Serves 4
Time 10–15 minutes

400g large shell-on king prawns, precooked or raw

3 baby gem lettuces

1 heaped tbsp finely chopped chives (plus optional extra to serve)

Pinch of smoked paprika or grated lime zest, to serve

For the dressing

3 tbsp olive oil

1 tbsp white wine vinegar

1 heaped tsp Dijon mustard

For the cocktail sauce

5 heaped tbsp mayonnaise (about 130g)

2 tsp tomato purée

1 tsp chipotle paste (or more if you like things extra hot)

½ tsp smoked paprika

Juice of 1 lime

1 tbsp Worcestershire sauce

Salt and freshly ground black pepper

If your prawns are raw, you'll need to cook them first. Either peel them, removing the heads but keeping the tails on and then boil them for 3–5 minutes until they turn pink. Or, keep the heads and tails on and fry them for a couple of minutes either side in a hot frying pan with a glug of oil (about 2 tbsp) until they are pink with a little golden colour. Set aside to cool.

Combine all the ingredients for the cocktail sauce in a bowl and season to taste. Refrigerate until ready to serve.

Separate the baby gem lettuce leaves and gently wash them. Drain, then tear any very large leaves.

In a large bowl, whisk together the oil, vinegar and mustard to make a dressing. Toss the lettuce leaves in the dressing together with the chives. Arrange the lettuce leaves on a serving platter or in individual bowls.

When ready to serve, spoon the cocktail sauce over the lettuce and top with the prawns. Finish with more chives, if you like, and a light dusting of smoked paprika or grated lime zest for a retro nod.

Do aheads

- The dressing can be made the day before and kept on the counter.
- The cocktail sauce can be made the day before and kept in the fridge.

Goes well with

- Simple soda bread p. 200
- New potatoes with anchovy chive butter p. 77

Chicory and pear seeded salad

This is the salad I turn to whenever I feel supper needs a lift and a green salad just will not do. It hits all the right notes of bitter, sweet, creamy and, most importantly, crunch. The dressing is a riff on my fennel seed vinaigrette (see page 186), which I lean on repeatedly, so I always have a bottle of sherry vinegar or – even better – moscatel vinegar in the cupboard. In a pinch, a good apple cider vinegar will also do.

Serves 4–6
Time 20 minutes

30g sunflower seeds
4 heads of red or white chicory or a mixture (about 350g)
30g Grana Padano or Parmesan
1 pear, ripe but still relatively firm (I like Williams pears)

For the dressing
1 tsp caraway seeds (or fennel seeds)
½ tsp coriander seeds
4 tbsp olive oil
1 tbsp moscatel vinegar or sherry vinegar
1 tbsp runny honey
Pinch of salt

In a dry frying pan set over a low heat, toast the sunflower seeds for 5–6 minutes or until they begin to turn golden and smell nutty. Transfer to a plate to cool.

In the same pan, lightly toast the caraway and coriander seeds over a low heat for 3 minutes or until they begin to smell fragrant. Transfer to a pestle and mortar and gently crush.

In a large bowl, combine the olive oil, vinegar, honey and salt to make the dressing. Whisk in the toasted caraway and coriander seeds.

Separate the chicory leaves and wash them, then drain and add them to the bowl.

Scatter in the toasted sunflower seeds and finely grate in about half of the Grana Padano or Parmesan using a Microplane grater. Toss to combine.

Core and thinly slice the pear, then add to the bowl and gently toss.

Transfer the salad to a serving plate and finish by generously grating over the remaining Grana Padano or Parmesan.

Do aheads
- The dressing can be made up to 3 days ahead and kept on the counter.
- The sunflower seeds can be toasted ahead.
- The chicory leaves can be separated and washed a few hours before serving (keep them refrigerated).

Goes well with
- Fennel, thyme and crème fraîche gratin **p. 124**
- Cider-braised chicken with apples **p. 127**
- Squash risotto with sage and pecan butter **p. 82**

Green beans with Pecorino and pine nuts

Green beans do not get enough airtime in my opinion. Too often reserved for the side of a plate or in the bottom righthand corner of a menu, rarely are they celebrated as the lead role. This is not a complicated recipe, but it is one that has never let me down. It has all the flavours of a pesto, only there is no blitzing involved – everything is left whole, lending the dish a rougher, more textured bite. Piled high onto a plate it looks quite spectacular.

Serves 4
Time 10 minutes

70g pine nuts
600g green beans, tops trimmed
1 small garlic clove, peeled
Grated zest of 1 unwaxed lemon
Juice of ½ lemon
Good pinch of salt
Olive oil
50g Pecorino (plus optional extra to serve)
Small bunch of basil (about 25g)

Toast the pine nuts first. Place a dry frying pan over a gentle heat and cook the pine nuts until lightly golden.

Bring a pan of salted water to the boil, then blanch the green beans for 2–3 minutes. Drain the beans while they are still crisp, then plunge them into ice-cold water to refresh. Drain again and pat dry with a clean tea towel.

Add the green beans to a large bowl and grate in the garlic and lemon zest. Squeeze in only half of the lemon juice at first. Add the salt and a generous glug of olive oil, then give everything a good toss.

Finely grate in the Pecorino, tear in the basil and scatter over the toasted pine nuts. Toss again. Taste to check the seasoning, adjusting with more lemon juice, olive oil or salt as necessary.

Transfer everything to a serving plate and finish with more grated Pecorino, if you like.

Do aheads

This comes together so quickly I rarely bother to make anything ahead, but when doubling-up the recipe to serve a crowd, I blanch the beans 2–3 hours before and keep in iced water until close to serving.

Goes well with

- Hake puttanesca **p. 105**
- Butterflied leg of lamb with red wine vinegar **p. 146**
- Crispy chicken thighs with lemon and pink peppercorns **p. 119**

Winter greens with almonds and figs

I have always had a deep appreciation for a good winter salad. Winter is usually the time of year when I crave nourishment the most and lean towards things that feel both fresh and healthy. This is one I make in various iterations throughout the cooler months, sometimes with cavolo nero, other times with curly kale or Savoy cabbage. The dressing is punchy so do not be alarmed if, when you taste it, it appears strong. Once the leaves are tossed through the dressing, the result is a flavourful, almost creamy salad with pops of crunch and sweetness from the roasted almonds and sticky dried figs. If you do not have time to roast a batch of almonds in the oven, a handful of flaked almonds toasted in a dry frying pan until golden work very well, too.

Serves 4
Time 15 minutes

400g cavolo nero (or curly kale or Savoy cabbage)

Olive oil

Pinch of coarse sea salt flakes

Juice of ½ lemon

120g dried figs, roughly chopped

75g roasted almonds, roughly chopped (or flaked almonds, toasted in a dry frying pan until golden)

75g Grana Padano or Parmesan, finely grated

For the dressing

30g tin of anchovies, plus their oil

50ml olive oil

Juice of 1 lemon (or more to taste)

75g Grana Padano or Parmesan, finely grated

Pull the cavolo nero or kale leaves from the stems, then roughly chop or tear the leaves with your hands. If using Savoy cabbage, roughly chop it into 2.5-cm pieces. Add to a large bowl with a good glug of olive oil, the sea salt flakes and lemon juice. Using your hands, massage the leaves for a minute or so to break them down slightly.

Next, make the dressing. Add the anchovies to a high-speed blender (I use a Nutribullet), along with the oil from the tin, the olive oil, lemon juice and grated Grana Padano or Parmesan. You will not need salt here as the anchovies bring enough with them. Blitz until smooth and glossy. Add more olive oil or lemon juice as needed – it should taste punchy and quite sharp.

Add the figs and almonds to the bowl with the cavolo nero. Drizzle over the dressing and give everything a good toss, scrunching the dressing in with your hands. Scatter over the grated Grana Padano or Parmesan and toss again. Transfer to a serving dish.

Goes well with
- Brothy beans with cavolo nero and chicken **p. 89**
- One-tray spatchcocked chicken with herby rice **p. 114**
- Squash risotto with sage and pecan butter **p. 82**

Bitter leaf salad with soft eggs

Bitter leaves have to be some of the best things about winter – even on the greyest of days, a bouquet of purply red leaves brings me an almost embarrassing level of joy. I love this salad as a mid-winter lunch and it always delivers whenever I am bored of anything soupy and instead want something fresh and crunchy. A handful of leftover roast chicken, feta or mozzarella is good in the place of the eggs, too. This salad also makes for an excellent addition to a bigger spread when the table needs an injection of colour.

Serves 3–6
Time 20 minutes

3 large eggs, at room temperature,
50g pumpkin seeds
1 large or 2 small heads of radicchio (or red chicory)
Small bunch of parsley (about 25g), leaves picked

For the dressing

2 tsp caraway seeds (or fennel, coriander or cumin seeds)
2 tbsp capers, rinsed and drained
2 tbsp red wine vinegar
6–7 tbsp olive oil
Grated zest of 1 unwaxed lemon
Juice of ½ lemon
Salt, to taste

Bring a pan of water to the boil. Lower in the eggs and boil for 7 minutes. After 7 minutes, scoop the eggs out of the pan and immediately plunge them into a bowl of ice-cold water. Let them cool for 5 minutes.

Meanwhile, in a dry frying pan set over a low heat, toast the pumpkin seeds for 2–3 minutes or until they begin to darken in colour and pop. Transfer to a plate to cool.

In the same pan, lightly toast the caraway seeds for the dressing over a low heat for 3 minutes or until they begin to smell fragrant. Transfer to a pestle and mortar and gently crush. Transfer directly into a large mixing bowl.

Using the flat of your knife, run the blade over the capers to roughly smoosh them, then add them to the bowl. Add the vinegar, olive oil, lemon zest and lemon juice to the bowl, then whisk well with a fork.

Using a sharp knife, thinly shred the radicchio. Wash and spin-dry the radicchio, then add to the bowl of dressing with the parsley leaves. Scatter in the toasted pumpkin seeds and give everything a good toss. Taste to check the seasoning, adjusting with more lemon juice, olive oil or some salt as necessary. Transfer everything to a serving plate.

When cool enough to handle, peel the boiled eggs. Halve or quarter the eggs and arrange them over the salad.

Do aheads

- The dressing can be made up to 3 days ahead and kept on the counter.
- The pumpkin seeds can be toasted ahead.

Goes well with

- Roast chicken (or any cold leftovers)
- New potatoes with anchovy chive butter **p.77**
- Potato rösti with fried eggs and soft herbs **p.62**

Za'atar cabbage, fennel, apple slaw

This is everything I want from a salad, especially during the cooler months when mealtimes can feel a bit stodgy and beige. It is one that comes with a big dose of flavour owing to the za'atar, which is filled with fragrant dried thyme and sumac. You can find za'atar in most supermarkets nowadays, otherwise look for it in good delis. I will often make this as a speedy, satisfying weeknight supper with some chicken or fish and it is also a very good one when cooking for friends. Once tossed, the slaw will hold its own for a good couple of hours – I will even go as far as saying that you can upturn any refrigerated leftovers the next day and present them with just as much glory and crunch as the day before. *Pictured on page 12.*

Serves 4–6
Time 10–15 minutes

60g sunflower seeds

1 small white cabbage (about 600g), finely shredded

1 fennel bulb, trimmed and thinly sliced

1 apple, cored and thinly sliced

Small bunch of mint (about 25g), leaves roughly chopped

Small bunch of parsley (about 25g), leaves roughly chopped

Small bunch of dill (about 25g), leaves roughly chopped

For the dressing

5 tbsp olive oil

Juice of 1 lemon

1 tbsp runny honey

1 small garlic clove, finely grated

Pinch of salt

2 tbsp za'atar

In a dry frying pan set over a low heat, toast the sunflower seeds for 5–6 minutes or until they begin to turn golden and smell nutty. Transfer to a plate to cool.

Next, make the dressing. Whisk all the ingredients for the dressing together in a large bowl.

Add the shredded cabbage and sliced fennel to the bowl with the dressing, then toss well. Add the sliced apple, chopped herbs and toasted sunflower seeds, then toss again and serve.

Do aheads

- The dressing can be made up to 3 days before and kept on the counter.
- The sunflower seeds can be toasted ahead.
- The cabbage can be shredded the day before and stored in a freezer bag or bowl in the fridge.

Goes well with

- Harissa sesame carrots with labneh **p. 95**
- Spiced aubergine on cold garlic yogurt **p. 71**
- Harissa honey chicken wings **p. 151**
- Roasted beetroot with whipped feta and green chilli salsa **p. 116**

Tomato salad

There are few things that say 'summer' more than a bright, vibrant tomato salad. The trick to the most flavourful tomato salad is to macerate the tomatoes by letting them sit for a while in a good pinch of salt. As they rest, the tomatoes release some of their flavourful juices, which make the base of the dressing for this salad. If you would like to keep this vegan, sub the tin of anchovies for an additional tablespoon of capers. *Pictured on page 149.*

Serves 4

Time 15 minutes, plus 20 minutes macerating time

800g ripe heritage tomatoes (or the best quality you can source)

Large pinch of coarse sea salt flakes

Small bunch of parsley (about 25g), leaves picked

For the dressing

30g tin of anchovies, drained

1 garlic clove

1 small banana shallot

1 tbsp capers, rinsed and drained

4 tbsp olive oil

2 tbsp moscatel vinegar or red wine vinegar

Halve or quarter the tomatoes and place them in a large colander set over a bowl to catch the juices. Toss the tomatoes with the sea salt and leave to macerate for 20 minutes. The tomatoes should soften slightly while releasing their juices, some of which will become the base of the dressing.

Finely chop the anchovies for the dressing. Peel and finely dice the garlic and shallot. Using the flat of your knife, roughly smoosh the capers. Add the anchovies, garlic, shallot and capers to a large bowl with the olive oil, vinegar and 3 tablespoons of the reserved tomato juices. Whisk everything together using a fork.

Finely chop the parsley leaves. Just before serving, toss the tomatoes and parsley through the dressing.

Goes well with
- Pan-fried courgettes with mozzarella and pistachio butter **p. 54**
- Crispy za'atar smashed potatoes **p. 96**
- Pan-fried seabass with olive salsa **p. 64**

FRIED

CHARRED ARTICHOKES
ON MINTY YOGURT
47

SPRINGTIME FRITTERS
49

AGRODOLCE AUBERGINES
51

PRAWN SAGANAKI
52

PAN-FRIED COURGETTES
WITH MOZZARELLA AND
PISTACHIO BUTTER
54

COURGETTE, ANCHOVY
AND LEMON FRITTI
57

PAN-FRIED CHICKEN WITH
CHILLI, TOMATOES AND MINT
58

HERBY MEATBALLS
WITH GREEN TAHINI
60

POTATO RÖSTI WITH FRIED
EGGS AND SOFT HERBS
62

CAVOLO NERO WITH
ANCHOVY, CHILLI
AND HAZELNUTS
63

PAN-FRIED SEABASS
WITH OLIVE SALSA
64

Despite the oily connotations the word 'fried' can conjure, some of my favourite meals have been cooked in my frying pan. When done right, the results are fresh, flavourful and light, but crucially they take very little time to cook and require virtually no washing up. They tend to be the recipes I make on repeat, especially during the week when I don't have as much time to cook but still want to eat something delicious. Most of the recipes in this chapter require a quick pan-fry as opposed to a deep fry, but it cannot be denied that some of the most delicious things are those that have had a little sizzle in some hot oil, so I've included some of my favourite 'deep-fried' ones, too. If, like I used to be, you're nervous of deep frying, I urge you to give it a go. It's easier than you think, and in the case of these recipes, does not require gallons of oil spluttering threateningly in a deep hot pan.

There are, however, two rules I encourage you to stick by when it comes to deep frying. Number one, try to ensure that whatever you are frying is as dry as possible before you dip it in the batter. Number two, have everything (and I mean everything) ready before you begin. There are many food writers and chefs who will probably tell you to use a food thermometer when frying to ensure that the oil is the exact temperature. I am sure they are right but I have never used a kitchen thermometer and find that most of the time the oil will change temperature as and when the wind changes, or when you add something to the pan, or when the doorbell rings. I have found frying most effective when I go by feel and look and that is how these recipes are written. I use a high-sided, wide, deep frying pan for most of my frying, the sort you might use for a risotto. I find it allows me to cook more at a time and really keep an eye on what is happening, too.

Charred artichokes on minty yogurt

I think of tinned artichokes as the Cinderellas of the artichoke world. In contrast to the glamorous and usually costly artichokes suspended in jars of olive oil, found in smart farm shops and Italian delis, tinned artichokes tend to be much more affordable. I first cooked this for a pot-luck supper with friends when I was a student and wanted to dress up the tinned artichokes with the same glossy splendour as her more extravagant step-sisters. It is a recipe I have cooked time and time again since. These are good served either cool or at room temperature, so feel free to make them ahead if you wish. I tend to pile them up on yogurt to eat with our fingers, but they make for a wonderful starter, side or sharing dish.

Serves 4–6
Time 15 minutes

2 x 400g tins of artichoke hearts in water, or use jarred artichokes in olive oil (500g drained weight for either type)
1 tsp dried oregano
Olive oil
Sea salt
Freshly squeezed lemon juice, to serve

For the minty yogurt
Handful of fresh mint
200g natural yogurt
1 small garlic clove, finely grated

Drain the artichokes and cut them in half lengthways. If the artichokes are tinned in water, add them to a bowl with a good glug of olive oil until well coated. If the artichokes are jarred in oil, simply add them to a bowl – there is no need to add more oil. Toss the artichokes with the dried oregano and a pinch of sea salt.

Pour in enough olive oil to coat the base of a large, heavy-based frying pan and set over a medium heat.

Arrange the artichokes, cut side down, in the pan and cook for about 4 minutes or until charred. Turn, then cook for a further 2–3 minutes.

While the artichokes are cooking, finely chop the mint and stir it into the yogurt with the garlic and a good pinch of sea salt.

Spoon the minty yogurt onto a serving plate and top with the charred artichokes. Squeeze over some fresh lemon juice and sprinkle over a little more sea salt, then serve.

Do aheads
- The yogurt can be prepared a day ahead and kept refrigerated.
- The artichokes can be charred a few hours ahead of time, then stored and served at room temperature.

Goes well with
- Asparagus and green bean mimosa salad **p. 15**
- Fruit and nut rice **p. 87**
- Wholegrain focaccia **p. 202**

Springtime fritters

These fritters are crispy, light and full of greens and, like most fritters, they are best enjoyed hot out of the pan with a pinch of flaky sea salt and a squeeze of fresh lemon juice. The batter is based on an Elizabeth David recipe that calls for a simple combination of flour, oil and water but with egg whites folded through just before frying. I find that a pinch of garlic powder and lots of cracked black pepper lends an additional layer of seasoning. The wild garlic brings a lot of flavour to these fritters, if you can get hold of it, but if you can't, some bold herbs work very well in its place. Basil and tarragon are my preference. A spider sieve is useful for these as it makes the process of transferring the fritters to a baking tray a bit smoother, however, metal tongs will do.

Serves 4–6
Time 30 minutes, plus 2 hours resting

- 250g asparagus, woody ends trimmed
- 150g Tenderstem broccoli
- 150g spring onions (about 2 bunches)
- 50g wild garlic (about 2 handfuls) or use a mix of basil and tarragon
- Grated zest of 2 unwaxed lemons
- 1 litre sunflower oil, for frying
- Lemon wedges, for squeezing over

For the batter
- 100g plain flour
- 2 tbsp olive oil
- 130–150ml warm water
- ½ tsp garlic powder
- Pinch of fine sea salt
- Plenty of cracked black pepper
- 4 large egg whites

First, make the batter. Sift the flour into a large bowl and make a well. Add the olive oil and stir it into the flour with a wooden spoon. Slowly add the warm water, stirring continuously, until it resembles double cream. Season with the garlic powder, salt and lots of cracked black pepper. Let the batter stand somewhere warm for at least 2 hours or until bubbles start to appear on the surface.

When ready to cook, roughly chop the asparagus, broccoli and spring onions into 1-cm pieces. When you reach the tips and florets, stop and just halve these lengthways. Add to a large bowl.

Roughly chop the wild garlic (or mixed herbs) and add to the bowl with the other vegetables. Grate in the lemon zest and stir to combine.

In a clean, grease-free bowl, whisk the egg whites until stiff using an electric whisk. Fold half of the whisked egg whites into the batter to loosen it, then gently fold in the remaining half.

Pour the sunflower oil into a wide, high-sided frying pan – it should reach at least 10cm up the sides of the pan – and set over a medium heat. To test the temperature of the oil, drop a little of the batter into the pan – once it starts to immediately sizzle, it is hot enough to cook. If you have a kitchen thermometer, aim for a constant oil temperature of 185–190°C. Keep a large baking tray lined with kitchen paper and a spider sieve nearby.

As the oil heats up, pour half of the batter onto the vegetables in the bowl and gently stir, then fold in the remaining batter – keep in as much air as you can.

Working in batches, carefully drop heaped tablespoons of the fritter mixture into the hot oil, ensuring there is a little space between each one (I tend to cook 4 or 5 at a time). They should instantly sizzle and spread a little as they cook – this is what makes them light and crispy. Cook for 5–6 minutes, turning with the tongs halfway through,

Continues »

until crisp and golden. Keep an eye on the oil temperature. If the fritters are browning too quickly, reduce the heat. Likewise, if they are taking longer to cook, increase the heat as you do not want soggy fritters. Trust your instinct here and remember the fritters will crisp up a touch further as they rest.

Pull one out when you think it is done. If you feel it could be crispier, leave the next ones for a little longer. Remove the fritters from the oil using the spider sieve and place on the kitchen paper-lined tray to drain. Season the fritters with sea salt flakes as soon as they come out of the pan. To keep them warm, cover loosely with foil.

Before serving, sprinkle a little more sea salt over the fritters. Serve with fat wedges of lemon for squeezing over.

Goes well with
- Fennel, shallot, tomato and garlic confit with burrata **p. 108**
- Artichoke, fennel and parmesan salad **p. 16**
- Chicken with saffron and chickpeas **p. 104**

Agrodolce aubergines

Agrodolce is an Italian term that means sour (*agro*) and sweet (*dolce*). It is a taste that I enjoy hugely and one of the main reasons I ensure I always have a well-stocked supply of vinegars. Different vinegars offer so much more than just acidity and can bring so much flavour to a dish. I use sherry vinegar in this, which has a delicious sour-sweetness. The aubergines drink up a good glug of it once cooked. The sun-blushed tomatoes add further sweetness to bounce off the capers. This salad is best enjoyed at room temperature and tastes even better the next day when the flavour intensifies. I love it as part of a medley of dishes, but it works very well as a condiment alondside some BBQ'd fish or meat, too.

Serves 4
Time 40 minutes

2 aubergines

2 tsp ground coriander

Olive oil

2 garlic cloves, finely chopped or crushed

2 tbsp sherry vinegar

50g sun-blushed tomatoes, roughly chopped

2 tbsp capers, rinsed and drained

Small bunch of parsley (about 25g), roughly chopped

Salt

Roughly chop the aubergines into 3-cm square chunks. Place in a large bowl with the ground coriander and a good pinch of salt, then toss to coat. Add a good glug of olive oil and toss again, ensuring all the aubergines are well coated.

Heat a large, non-stick pan over a medium heat. Working in two batches, cook the aubergines for about 10 minutes, tossing every so often until browned on all sides. Once browned, return all the aubergines to the pan and continue to cook over a gentle heat for 5 minutes or until softened and cooked through.

With the heat on low, add a little more olive oil to the pan along with the garlic and cook for about 2 minutes. Add the vinegar, sun-blushed tomatoes and capers and cook for a further minute or so. Season to taste with salt. Switch off the heat and allow the aubergines to cool slightly.

When you are ready to serve, stir through the chopped parsley along with another glug of olive oil. Taste to check the seasoning, adjusting as necessary.

Goes well with
- Prawn saganaki **p. 52**
- Filo baked feta with harissa and honey **p. 98**
- Za'atar cabbage, fennel, apple slaw **p. 40**

Prawn saganaki

My favourite place in all the world is a small island called Spetses, situated just off mainland Greece. Whenever we visit, our first supper is always at a taverna called Bouboulina, where we order the prawn saganaki. The recipe is a family secret but it begins with a rich fish stock. All day, a huge silver pot bubbles on the stove enriched with shellfish shells, and it is this that makes the Bouboulina prawn saganaki so special. Inspired by Bouboulina, I start my own prawn saganaki by making a very quick chilli-spiked fish stock of sorts with the shells from the prawns. A key part of a classic prawn saganaki is ouzo, but it can be hard to come by in the UK, so I add toasted fennel seeds and tarragon to mine, which have a similar aniseed taste to ouzo. The result is perhaps not quite as good as the original, but very delicious all the same.

Serves 4
Time 50 minutes

12 raw king prawns, shell on
1 tsp fennel seeds
Olive oil
400g cherry tomatoes
4 spring onions, finely chopped
½ tsp chilli flakes
1 garlic clove, peeled
400g tin of chopped tomatoes
100g feta
30g tarragon, leaves picked and finely chopped

For the prawn stock

3 tbsp olive oil
1 garlic clove, thinly sliced
1 tsp chilli flakes

Devein and shell the prawns, removing their heads but leaving their tails on. Set aside the shells and heads for the stock.

Next, make the prawn stock. Heat the olive oil in a medium saucepan. Add the sliced garlic and chilli flakes along with the reserved prawn shells and heads. Gently fry for about 5 minutes or until the shells have gained some colour. Using a wooden spoon, crush the shells to release the flavour. Add 150ml of water and allow the mixture to gently simmer and reduce for 10 minutes.

Strain the liquid through a sieve, squishing out as much as you can. You should be left with about 100ml of prawn stock. Set aside.

Heat a large, dry frying pan over a low heat and cook the fennel seeds for a couple of minutes until they smell fragrant, then set aside.

Add a glug of olive oil to the pan along with the cherry tomatoes. Give the pan a shake to coat the tomatoes in the oil, then cook over a medium-high heat, shaking the pan every so often, for 5 minutes or until the tomatoes begin to char.

Reduce the heat to medium, add the fennel seeds, spring onions and chilli flakes, then crush or finely grate in the garlic clove. Tossing everything in the pan, cook for a further 3 minutes or until the spring onions have softened.

Add the prawn stock and tinned tomatoes to the pan and bring everything to a vigorous simmer for 7–10 minutes or until the tomatoes have reduced and thickened.

Crumble in half the feta and scatter over half the chopped tarragon. Stir until the feta has begun to break down and melt into the sauce.

Add the prawns to the pan, tossing them so they are as well coated in the sauce as possible. Cook for 1–2 minutes, depending on their size. Turn them and cook for a further minute until pink. Switch off the heat. Top with the remaining crumbled feta and tarragon, and serve.

Goes well with

- Salsa verde salad **p. 25**
- Agrodolce aubergines **p. 51**
- Wholegrain flatbreads **p. 199**

Pan-fried courgettes with mozzarella and pistachio butter

I can never get enough of courgettes when in season but they can get a bit of a hard time for being a watery vegetable and it is true, they are. I find the best way to cook them is either to lean into their wateriness by cooking them gently and slowly, or cooking them over a brisk, high heat. Here they are pan-fried in under 10 minutes until their outsides are golden but their insides retain a good bite. It is not complicated and a good way to free up some space in the oven or BBQ where they will take longer to cook. The char of the pan brings out the natural sweetness in the courgettes, which marries perfectly with the chilli-spiked, herby butter and milky mozzarella. Always tear your mozzarella instead of cutting it. Not only does it look better, I find the creaminess is amplified when served this way.

Serves 4–6
Time 25 minutes

5 medium courgettes (about 750g)
Olive oil
Pinch of salt
150g ball of mozzarella

For the pistachio chilli herb butter

75g butter
1 garlic clove, finely grated
1 tsp chilli flakes
50g pistachios, roughly chopped
1 tbsp finely chopped parsley leaves
1 tbsp finely chopped mint leaves
Pinch of coarse sea salt

Roughly cut the courgettes into 2-cm thick rounds. Toss in a bowl with a good glug of olive oil and pinch of salt.

Heat a thin layer of olive oil in a heavy-based pan. Working in batches, add a single layer of courgette to the pan, arranging them cut side down, and cook for 3–4 minutes on either side until golden and charred. They should still have a bit of bite in the middle. Repeat with the rest of the courgette slices.

Meanwhile, melt the butter in a saucepan with the grated garlic and chilli flakes. Switch off the heat, stir through the chopped pistachios, herbs and a pinch of coarse salt, then allow it to sit for 5 minutes.

Arrange the courgettes on a serving plate, tear over the mozzarella and spoon over the butter, then serve.

Do aheads

You can cook the courgettes a few hours ahead of time and enjoy them at room temperature. I often add all the butter ingredients to the saucepan a couple of hours ahead, too, so that all I have to do is whack it on the heat for a few minutes before serving.

Goes well with

- Saffron butter beans **p. 85**
- Herb salad with crushed hazelnuts **p. 18**
- Wholegrain flatbreads **p. 199**

Courgette, anchovy and lemon fritti

I will always order courgette fritti whenever I see it on a menu, but they are not difficult to recreate at home, with all the components taking just minutes to prepare. There is no need for a deep-fat fryer or any other fancy equipment, although a slotted spoon or spider sieve is useful. I find a wide frying pan easier to manage than a deep saucepan for this as it is easier to see what you are doing, and you can fry more at a time. Using a vegetable peeler to get the strips of courgette means that you will always achieve evenly thin pieces. The best fritti are the ones that curl round in the pan and go extra crispy. I love the added saltiness of anchovies and bitter-sweet lemon, but you can stick to just courgette, if you wish.

Serves 4–6
Time 30 minutes

3 small courgettes

30g tin of anchovies

1 unwaxed lemon (plus extra wedges to serve)

1 litre sunflower or vegetable oil, for frying

For the batter

100g plain flour

60g cornflour

Pinch of fine sea salt (plus extra for the fritti)

200–250ml sparkling water, ice-cold from the fridge

Using a vegetable peeler or sharp knife, roughly slice the courgettes into 4-mm strips and place in a bowl. Drain the anchovies. Cut the lemon into thin slices. Set aside.

In a large mixing bowl, whisk together the flours and salt for the batter. Slowly add the chilled sparkling water, whisking as you do so, until you have a thick batter that resembles double cream.

Pour the oil into a wide, heavy-based pan and set over a medium heat. To test the temperature of the oil, drop a torn piece of bread into the pan – once it starts to sizzle, it is hot enough to cook. Keep a large baking tray lined with kitchen paper ready and a pair of tongs and a spider sieve nearby. If available, set the oven to 60°C fan to keep the fritti warm.

Working in batches, drop the courgette pieces into the batter. Shake off any excess batter, then carefully drop them into the hot oil. Cook for 3 minutes, turning with tongs halfway through. Remove the fritti from the oil using the spider sieve and place on the lined baking tray to drain. Season the fritti with salt as soon as they come out of the pan. To keep them warm, cover loosely with foil or place in the warm oven, if available.

Once all the courgette fritti are cooked, coat the anchovies in the batter and cook in the same way. Do the same with the lemon slices.

Pile all the fritti onto a serving plate and serve with fresh lemon wedges for squeezing over.

Goes well with

- Gnudi with roasted tomato sauce **p. 112**
- Nectarines with burrata and pink peppercorns **p. 20**
- Wholegrain focaccia **p. 202**

Pan-fried chicken with chilli, tomatoes and mint

I often turn to this recipe when I fancy something that feels a bit special but does not require too much effort. It is both delicious and substantial, but crucially does not demand much washing up. Everything is tossed together in the one bowl before being cooked together in a single pan. The chicken gets a bit of a char while the tomatoes almost collapse upon themselves, creating a sticky, jammy sauce. The chilli gives the dish a good kick, which suits me well, but you can go easy on the chilli if you are sensitive to spice. Enjoy this alongside a quick green salad or some well-dressed, crunchy, blanched greens, and some steamed rice, if you like.

Serves 4 (or 2 hungry people)
Time 30 minutes,
plus 20 minutes marinating

600g skinless, boneless chicken thighs
175g baby plum or cherry tomatoes
Pinch of salt

For the marinade
4 tbsp olive oil
2 garlic cloves, crushed or finely grated
Juice of 1 lemon (plus extra to serve)
1 tsp chilli flakes (or ½ tsp if you are sensitive to heat)
2 tbsp finely chopped mint leaves (plus extra leaves to garnish)

Combine the olive oil, garlic, lemon juice, chilli flakes and chopped mint for the marinade in a large bowl. Add the chicken thighs and toss well to coat. Leave to marinate for 20 minutes outside of the fridge, or refrigerate overnight and then bring to room temperature 20 minutes before cooking.

Pierce the tomatoes with a sharp knife – this prevents them from splitting too early on. Add these to the bowl with the chicken just before cooking and give everything a quick mix to coat the tomatoes in the marinade.

Heat a large frying pan over a medium heat. Add the chicken thighs and tomatoes to the pan, spacing out the chicken evenly. Cook for about 8–10 minutes on either side, lightly shaking the pan every so often. The chicken is done when cooked through, golden brown and slightly sticky, while the tomatoes should have charred in places and collapsed in on themselves. Switch off the heat, add a good pinch of salt and allow the chicken to rest in the pan for a further 5–10 minutes.

Transfer the chicken to a serving platter or plates. Using a spatula or wooden spoon, scrape any caramelised stickiness that has collected on the base of the pan as you scoop up the tomatoes to spoon over the chicken. Finish with some extra mint leaves.

Do aheads
You can marinate the chicken a day ahead. Just remember to bring it to room temperature before cooking to ensure tender meat.

Goes well with
- Salsa verde salad **p. 25**
- Green beans with Pecorino and pine nuts **p. 34**
- Winter greens with almonds and figs **p. 37**

Herby meatballs with green tahini

If you are thinking of classic Italian meatballs in a slow-cooked tomato sauce, these are not that. They are light, zesty and full of herbs and are what I make when I am in need of a speedy supper as they require little preparation. I tend to make them on a whim, picking up the meat and herbs on my way home. The spices are ones always found in my cupboard, and hopefully in yours, too. The za'atar is not essential but it is a lovely addition and can be found in most supermarkets these days. My husband loves these meatballs folded into a wrap or flatbread, while I love them with a zippy salad or crunchy slaw. The green tahini is a must and can be whizzed up in no time.

Serves 4
Time 30 minutes

For the meatballs

500g lean beef mince (or use coarse or turkey mince)

1 red onion, grated using the coarse side of a box grater

2 fat garlic cloves, finely grated

Grated zest of 1 unwaxed lemon

1 tsp ground cumin

½ tsp ground cinnamon

½ tsp ground coriander

2 tsp za'atar (or increase the ground coriander to 2 tsp)

1 heaped tsp coarse sea salt flakes

Small bunch of dill (approx. 25g), finely chopped, plus an extra handful to serve

Handful of mint leaves (approx. 15g), finely chopped, plus an extra handful to serve

Handful of parsley (approx. 15g), roughly chopped, plus an extra handful to serve

Olive oil

To serve

Green tahini (**p. 188**)

Freshly squeezed lemon juice, plus extra wedges

Do aheads

- The meatballs can be prepared up to a day ahead and kept refrigerated.
- The green tahini can be made up to 3 days ahead, kept refrigerated and then brought to room temperature before serving.

These meatballs take no time at all to make, so I tend to prepare the green tahini first (see page 188).

To make the meatballs, place all the ingredients, except the olive oil, in a large bowl. Using your hands, mix everything together well, breaking down the mince and ensuring all the ingredients are evenly distributed. Divide the mixture into four, then divide each quarter further into four evenly-sized meatballs. Compress each one a few times in your hands before shaping them into an even round. You will end up with 16 meatballs.

Heat 2–3 tablespoons of olive oil in a large frying pan over a medium-low heat. Once the oil is shimmering, add the meatballs to the pan. You may need to cook them in batches. Cook the meatballs for about 4 minutes, turning them regularly so they cook evenly. You are looking for the meatballs to brown but not char. Once they are seared all over, reduce the heat to the lowest level and cook for a further 4 minutes, gently shaking the pan every so often.

Spoon most of the green tahini onto a serving plate, then top with the meatballs. Squeeze over some fresh lemon juice, add a drizzle of olive oil and scatter over the extra herbs. Serve with fresh lemon wedges for squeezing over and any remaining green tahini on the side.

Goes well with

- Za'atar cabbage, fennel, apple slaw **p. 40**
- Loaded feta with peach, olives and herbs **p. 28**
- Wholegrain focaccia **p. 202**

Potato rösti with fried eggs and soft herbs

Rösti is a popular Swiss dish made with grated potato and sometimes onions, squashed into a patty and fried in a pan until golden and crisp. It is somewhere between a potato pancake and a giant hash brown. I lived in Switzerland for about a year as a child and one of the best parts was eating rösti. It is something that I make regularly at home as a comforting quick supper. I love it with fried eggs, which cook quickly in the still-hot pan while the rösti gets sliced down the middle and slid onto plates. It also makes for a very good pre-dinner snack. Cut it into wedges and and serve with a spoonful of crème fraîche, labneh or ricotta and some chopped chives or even half a soft-boiled egg.

Serves 2 or 4
Time 40 minutes

For the rösti
700g King Edward or Maris Piper potatoes
Good pinch of sea salt flakes
50g butter
4 tbsp olive oil

To serve
2–4 eggs
Crème fraîche (or use labneh or whipped ricotta) (optional)
Small handful of chives, finely snipped (or roughly chopped mixed fresh herbs, such as parsley, mint and dill)
Freshly cracked black pepper

Peel the potatoes. Using the large holes of a box grater, grate the potatoes into a bowl. Rinse thoroughly with cold water, swirling the grated potato to release the starch, then draining and refreshing until the water runs clear.

Transfer the drained grated potato to a clean tea towel, then squeeze to remove as much water as possible. Dry the bowl. Return the potato to the bowl and season with sea salt, then stir.

Melt half the butter with 2 tablespoons of the olive oil in a frying pan over a medium-low heat. Add the grated potato to the pan. While pressing down as lightly as possible, shape the potato into an even layer, tucking in the sides to make a neat round. Cook for about 5 minutes or until you can feel that a crisp base has just started to form when you gently shake the pan. Reduce the heat and cook for a further 4–5 minutes. Using your spatula, gently lift an edge of the rösti to check that it has gained a golden colour.

Take either a small wooden chopping board or medium plate. Place it on top of the rösti and – taking care not to touch the edge of the pan – confidently flip the pan over so the board or plate is now underneath. Lift off the pan and return it to the heat. Melt the remaining butter with the remaining olive oil and slide the rösti back into the pan, then cook over the lowest heat on the other side for a further 5–10 minutes or until the rösti has cooked through.

If serving the rösti with fried eggs for two, divide the rösti down the middle in the pan and slide one half onto each plate. The pan will still be warm so crank up the heat and fry the eggs to your liking.

If serving the rösti with soft-boiled eggs for four to share, divide the rösti into four in the pan and slide a quarter onto each plate. Meanwhile, cook either 2 or 4 eggs in boiling water for 6 minutes, then plunge them immediately into ice-cold water. Once cool enough to handle, peel the eggs, then slice in half. Nestle the eggs on top of the rösti with a spoonful of crème fraîche, some snipped chives and some freshly cracked black pepper.

Goes well with
- Herb salad with crushed hazelnuts **p. 18**
- Artichoke, fennel and parmesan salad **p. 16**

Cavolo nero with anchovy, chilli and hazelnuts

Winter greens love anchovy and chilli. I like to use cavolo nero for this, but regular kale or purple sprouting broccoli are equally delicious when prepared this way. It makes for a delicious side, but it also works well as more of a sharing dish if you tear over some mozzarella or add a beautiful blob of burrata. I'll also enjoy this for a midweek lunch, either tossed through some pasta or rice, or just as it is.

Serves 4–6
Time 15 minutes

30g roasted hazelnuts, roughly chopped
300g cavolo nero
Olive oil
2 garlic cloves, finely grated
1 tsp chilli flakes
30g tin anchovies, drained and roughly chopped
Sea salt (optional)

If the hazelnuts are not already roasted, scatter them over a dry baking tray, place in an oven preheated to 180°C fan and roast for 10 minutes. Allow to cool, then roughly chop or crush the hazelnuts by wrapping them in a clean tea towel and gently rolling over them with a rolling pin.

Starting at the woody end, pull the leaves from the stems of the cavolo nero. Discard the stems (or keep them for making a stock). Roughly chop the leaves into 3-cm pieces – there is no need to be precise about this.

Heat a good glug of olive oil in a large frying pan over a low heat. Add the garlic, chilli flakes and chopped anchovies, then cook for a minute or so, moving the mixture around the pan with a wooden spoon until the anchovies start to break down.

Add the cavolo nero to the pan and toss the leaves in the anchovy mixture – using tongs is best for this. Cook for about 5 minutes or until the cavolo nero has wilted and softened. Switch off the heat. Add the chopped hazelnuts and another glug of olive oil, then toss again. Taste to check the seasoning. The anchovies are naturally salty, so you may not need to add any salt at all.

Do aheads

The hazelnuts can be roasted and chopped ahead of time.

Goes well with

- Baked salmon with blood orange and chilli **p. 122**
- Crispy chicken thighs with lemon and pink peppercorns **p. 119**
- Gnudi with roasted tomato sauce **p. 112**

Pan-fried seabass with olive salsa

Whenever I chat to people about cooking, it is often the prospect of cooking fish that strikes the most fear in the kitchen. There seems to be great concern about potentially undercooking fish, while most of us do not get in the same head-spin at the thought of undercooking chicken, yet the consequences would be equally – if not more – disastrous. In fact, pan-frying fish is an incredibly simple way to cook fish and there really is little that can go wrong. The key is to oil the fish properly and apply a bit of pressure once it is added to the pan. This is how you achieve a crispy skin and, honestly, if you lose a little skin during the flipping process, just blame the spatula and patch it up with some salsa.

Serves 2–4
Time 25 minutes

4 seabass fillets
Olive oil
Sea salt
Lemon wedges, to serve

For the salsa

200g pitted green olives
2 tbsp capers, rinsed and drained
Olive oil
1 garlic clove, finely sliced
Pinch of sugar
40g roasted blanched almonds (preferably marcona almonds), roughly chopped
Small bunch of parsley (about 25g), roughly chopped
1 tbsp roughly chopped mint leaves
Freshly squeezed lemon juice (about 1 tbsp)

First, make the salsa. Either tear the olives or use the blade of a knife to squash them. Set aside on your chopping board or transfer to a bowl. Squash the capers, running the knife over them a few times.

Heat 2 tablespoons of olive oil in a small frying pan or saucepan over a low heat. Add the garlic and cook for a couple of minutes or until it begins to soften and smell fragrant. Add the squashed olives and capers to the pan along with the sugar, then gently cook for 5 minutes or until warmed through. Add the almonds and cook for a further minute. Switch off the heat, then stir through the herbs. Add another glug of olive oil along with the lemon juice. Taste to check the seasoning. Set aside and cover to keep warm.

Pat the seabass fillets dry with kitchen paper, then season with olive oil and sea salt. Add about 1 tablespoon of olive oil to a frying pan set over a medium-high heat. Once the oil is hot, add the seabass fillets, skin side down. Using a spatula, gently press the fish down (this helps the skin to crisp) and cook for 5 minutes. Flip over the fish and cook on the other side for a further 1–2 minutes. If you are cooking the fillets two at a time, either transfer the first two to a baking tray or plate and cover in foil, or pop them into a preheated oven set to 70°C fan to keep warm.

When ready to serve, spoon the warm salsa over the seabass fillets and serve with fresh lemon wedges for squeezing over.

Do aheads

The salsa can be made ahead of time and kept in a pan, then reheated till warm just before serving.

Goes well with

- New potatoes with anchovy chive butter (also pictured opposite) **p. 77**
- Tomato salad **p. 41**
- Cavolo nero with anchovy, chilli and hazelnuts **p. 63**

STIRRED

**SPICED AUBERGINE
ON COLD GARLIC YOGURT**
71

**CRAB, PRAWN AND
TOMATO SPAGHETTI**
73

**STICKY LEMONY
COURGETTE RICE**
74

**NEW POTATOES WITH
ANCHOVY CHIVE BUTTER**
77

**SOFT COURGETTES WITH
CHICKPEAS, LEMON AND
MINT**
78

**PAPPARDELLE WITH
WALNUTS, NUTMEG
AND LEMON**
80

**SQUASH RISOTTO WITH
SAGE AND PECAN BUTTER**
82

SAFFRON BUTTER BEANS
85

RED WINE-BRAISED LENTILS
86

FRUIT AND NUT RICE
87

**BROTHY BEANS WITH
CAVOLO NERO AND CHICKEN**
89

I moved a lot while studying in my twenties and for almost a year I lived without an oven. We had a small fridge and a double ring hob, the sort that you can plug in anywhere and move around. I loved that hob. I cooked a lot on that hob. For the first two months, I think I existed purely on porridge and stir-fries, until I grew tired of supermarket ready-shredded vegetables and looked for inspiration elsewhere. One of the things I started cooking lots of during this time were pulses and beans. In a bid to vary things up, I quickly learnt that a tiny pinch of saffron could turn a can of butter beans into something quite different, or that crisping up some rosemary or sage gave a modest bean stew an entirely new character, both in look and flavour. Almost all of these recipes can be enjoyed as they are as the sole entity of a meal, and many of them work as part of a bigger cast. There are one or two that perhaps take on the role of more obvious sides, but as is the case with many recipes, they are made instantly more robust with the addition of a crispy fried or jammy egg.

Spiced aubergine on cold garlic yogurt

Sitting somewhere between a stew and a dip, this spiced aubergine has more of a warming heat as opposed to a punchy kick, with the dates bringing a subtle sweetness. I love to serve this with some good bread or flatbreads as a starter, or alongside a medley of salads. I like it best slightly warm, but I also think it tastes even better the next day and so I tend to make it ahead, then warm it through just before serving. The coolness of the garlicky yogurt is perfect with the sticky tomato and really benefits from a few hours in the fridge to take on the garlicky flavour.

Serves 4–6
Time 1 hour 20 minutes

3 large aubergines
Sea salt
Olive oil
1 red onion, finely sliced
2 heaped tbsp harissa paste
2 tsp mixed spice
2 tbsp tomato purée
2 large tomatoes, roughly chopped
400g tin of chopped tomatoes
5 Medjool dates, stoned and roughly chopped

For the garlic yogurt
200g full-fat Greek yogurt
1 small garlic clove, peeled
Coarse sea salt flakes

Spoon the yogurt into a bowl. Finely grate the garlic into the yogurt using a Microplane grater, then stir in a good pinch of sea salt. Allow the yogurt to chill in the fridge for at least a couple of hours.

Preheat the oven to 200°C fan. Line two large baking trays with parchment paper.

Chop the aubergines into roughly 3-cm large chunks. Place in a bowl with a good pinch of sea salt and a generous amount of olive oil, then toss to coat, ensuring all the aubergines are well coated. Arrange over the two lined trays and cook in the oven for 25–30 minutes or until browned on all sides. Rotate the trays halfway through for an even cook.

Meanwhile, heat a large glug of olive oil in a deep, heavy-based saucepan or casserole dish over a low heat. Add the onion and cook for 10–12 minutes or until softened. Add the harissa, mixed spice and tomato purée and cook for a further 2–3 minutes before adding the chopped fresh tomatoes, tinned tomatoes and the dates. Fill the tomato tin with water and add that too. Stir to combine and allow the mixture to simmer for 20 minutes, stirring every so often. The sauce should be thick and glossy – the tomatoes and dates should have mostly broken down.

Transfer the cooked aubergines to the pan with the sauce, stir to combine and cook over a low heat for a further 5–10 minutes or until the aubergines have cooked through. Taste to check the seasoning and adjust as needed.

Spoon the garlic yogurt onto a serving plate and pile the spiced aubergine mixture on top.

Do aheads
- You can roast the aubergines ahead of time to free up oven space.
- The garlic yogurt can also be made up to 2 days ahead and stored in the fridge.
- I think this tastes even better the next day, so try to make the entire thing a day ahead if time allows.

Goes well with
- Wholegrain flatbreads p. 199
- Fruit and nut rice p. 87
- Filo baked feta with harissa and honey p. 98

Crab, prawn and tomato spaghetti

Seafood pasta always feels celebratory. It reminds me of holidays by the sea, relaxed, messy lunches and tomato-stained paper tablecloths. If I'm making this dish for friends, I serve it on a huge platter brought to the table for everyone to help themselves, which means everyone can take as much as they like. I love tarragon in this, especially with the crab, but if you are not a fan, feel free to use parsley instead.

Serves 4
Time 35 minutes

8 large raw king prawns, shell on
Olive oil
2–3 tsp chilli flakes
350g dried spaghetti
2 shallots or 1 banana shallot, finely chopped
4 garlic cloves, finely chopped
150g cherry tomatoes
Large glass (250ml) of dry white wine
200g white crab meat
Small bunch of tarragon, approx. 25g (or parsley) (plus optional extra leaves to serve)
Grated zest of 1 unwaxed lemon
50g butter
Juice of ½ lemon
Sea salt and freshly cracked black pepper

Devein and shell the prawns, removing their heads. Set aside the shells and heads for the stock. Roughly chop the prawns and set aside.

Make the prawn stock. Heat 6 tablespoons of olive oil in a medium saucepan over a medium heat. Add the reserved prawn shells and heads with 1 teaspoon of the chilli flakes, then pour in 200ml of water. Cook for about 10 minutes. Using a wooden spoon, crush the shells and heads to release the flavour. Once the prawn heads are cooked through and the stock is vibrant red, take off the heat. Strain the liquid through a sieve into a bowl. Discard the shells and heads.

Check the packet instructions to gauge the cooking time for the spaghetti. The next stage takes 10 minutes in total, so you may want to get the pasta on now. If so, bring a large pan of salted water to the boil and cook the spaghetti according to the packet instructions.

In a separate large, heavy-based pan, heat a further 3 tablespoons of olive oil over a gentle heat. Add the finely chopped shallots and garlic along with the remaining chilli flakes – use less if you're sensitive to spice. Cook for 5 minutes or until the shallots and garlic are soft.

Add the tomatoes to the pan, then shake them about a bit to coat them in the oil. Increase the heat ever so slightly and cook the tomatoes until they begin to burst – you can use the back of your spoon to help them along.

Add the wine and prawn stock to the pan, then allow it to come to a lively simmer.

Stir through the chopped prawns, allowing them to cook for just 30 seconds – they will cook very quickly. Next, fold in the crab meat, then add the cooked and drained spaghetti, the tarragon leaves, lemon zest and butter. Toss everything together well. Squeeze in half of the lemon juice and add a good pinch of salt. Taste to check the seasoning, adding more lemon juice, if you like.

To serve, drizzle over some good-quality olive oil and season with plenty of freshly cracked black pepper. Scatter over more tarragon leaves, if you like.

Goes well with
- Tomato salad **p. 41**
- Charred spring onions with burrata, peas and dill **p. 143**

Sticky lemony courgette rice

I think of this almost as a lazy risotto. It's stickier and has a bit more bite, but the key difference is that there is no need to stand by the hob continuously stirring. Some effort is required at the beginning as the base consists of very thinly sliced, slow-cooked courgettes. These cook first until almost caramelised, but after that they need minimal attention. In fact, in my opinion, if they catch and burn a little, they're even more delicious. Once the courgettes are done, you can pretty much walk away as the rice cooks slowly with thick lemon rind, stock and softened spring onions until the grains are plump with flavour. Give it all one good stir and finish with a tumble of herbs. I love to serve this alongside a good roast chicken or even a BBQ, but it makes for a brilliant main course, too.

Serves 4–6
Time 1 hour 10 minutes

- 50g toasted pine nuts
- 3 courgettes
- 1 unwaxed lemon
- Olive oil
- Sea salt
- Bunch of spring onions, chopped into 5-mm pieces
- 2 garlic cloves, peeled
- 400g short-grain brown rice
- 500ml stock (either chicken or vegetable)
- Generous handful of basil leaves

If your pine nuts are not yet toasted, do this first by cooking them in a dry frying pan over a gentle heat until golden brown. Allow to cool.

Thinly slice the courgettes into rounds about 3-mm thick.

Using a sharp knife, slice away thick pieces of the lemon rind so that you are left with the fruit. Set both the rind and the fruit aside.

Heat a good glug of olive oil – enough to coat the base – in a heavy-based saucepan set over a medium heat. Add the courgettes to the pan with a pinch of sea salt. Avoid touching the courgettes for the first 4 minutes to allow them to colour on the bottom, then reduce the heat and toss the courgettes occasionally until most of them are browned and caramelised – this will take 5–10 minutes. Transfer to a bowl and set aside.

Add the chopped spring onions to the pan, adding a little more oil if needed, and cook for 2 minutes. Finely grate in the garlic and cook for a further minute or so.

Add the rice to the pan with the stock and lemon rind. Stir to combine, bring the rice to the boil, then reduce to a simmer. Cover and cook for 45 minutes or until the stock has been absorbed. Stir the rice once or twice partway through the cooking time.

Once the liquid has just been absorbed and the rice is cooked, return the courgettes to the pan. Add the basil leaves, the squeezed juice from the lemon and a good pinch of sea salt along with another glug of olive oil. Stir to combine.

Transfer everything to a serving plate and scatter over the toasted pine nuts.

Goes well with
- Asparagus and green bean mimosa salad **p. 15**
- Herb salad with crushed hazelnuts **p. 18**
- Crispy chicken thighs with lemon and pink peppercorns **p. 119**

New potatoes with anchovy chive butter

Buttery new potatoes will always bring joy to the table, and these are a wonderful accompaniment to practically anything. The butter takes on an almost umami creaminess thanks to a tin of anchovies. While they add a richness to the flavour, the actual anchovy taste is subtle here as the cooking process mellows out their punch. Even if you are not a fan of anchovies, I do recommend trying them in this.

Serves 4
Time 35 minutes

750g new potatoes
45g tin anchovies in oil
1 garlic clove, finely grated
50g butter
Grated zest and juice of 1 unwaxed lemon
Small bunch of chives (about 20g), finely chopped
Sea salt

Bring a large saucepan of salted water to the boil. Halve any larger potatoes, then add all of them to the pan. Boil the potatoes for 15–25 minutes or until tender, then drain and set aside.

Return the saucepan to the heat. Open the tin of anchovies over the pan in order to catch the oil in the pan. Then roughly chop the anchovies and add to the pan along with the grated garlic. Cook over a gentle heat until the anchovies have broken down.

Add the butter to the pan. Once the butter has melted, add the grated zest of the lemon and about a quarter of its juice. Stir until slightly emulsified.

Return the potatoes to the pan along with the chives, then stir until well coated, allowing some of them to crush under the weight of the spatula as you toss them in the butter. As the anchovies are already salty, add just a pinch of salt and toss again. Taste to check the seasoning, adjusting with more lemon juice or salt as needed. Serve immediately while hot.

Goes well with
- Pan-fried seabass with olive salsa (also pictured opposite) **p. 64**
- Pan-fried chicken with chilli, tomatoes and mint **p. 58**
- Hake puttanesca **p. 105**
- Grilled bream with charred spring onion salsa **p. 147**

Soft courgettes with chickpeas, lemon and mint

This courgette dish reminds me of high summer when it is warm enough to sit outside in just a t-shirt and the evenings stay light long past 8pm. I love to eat outside when the weather is like this and often make this as a midweek supper, foregoing a set table and propping the bowl up on my knees on the outdoor steps to enjoy with a glass of rosé. Try to look for good-quality chickpeas in a jar if you can. Their preserving stock is what brings the glossy soupiness to this, so make sure you don't drain them. The quantities given below will serve two as the main event, or four when served with some other things.

Serves 2–4
(as a main meal or a sharing dish)
Time 25 minutes

Olive oil
2 garlic cloves, crushed
2 courgettes, thinly sliced
Coarse sea salt flakes
700g jar of chickpeas, including their liquid
40g Grana Padano or Parmesan, finely grated
Grated zest of 1 unwaxed lemon
Juice from up to ½ lemon
Small bunch of mint (about 25g), leaves finely chopped
Freshly cracked black pepper
Crème fraîche, natural yogurt or ricotta, to serve

Heat a good glug of olive oil in a frying pan over a gentle heat. Add the garlic and cook for 2 minutes. Add the courgettes with a large pinch of sea salt and cook for 6–8 minutes or until softened enough that they are flopping and folding over themselves.

Pour the chickpeas into the pan along with their liquid from the jar, scatter in the Grana Padano or Parmesan and cook for about 5 minutes or until the chickpeas have warmed through and the sauce has thickened and emulsified slightly. Switch off the heat. Stir through the lemon zest, just a squeeze of lemon juice and the chopped mint, along with another good pinch of salt. Taste to check the seasoning, adjusting as needed. Drizzle over more olive oil and finish with some freshly cracked black pepper.

Divide the courgette and chickpea mixture between bowls and serve with a spoonful of crème fraîche, natural yogurt or ricotta, if you like.

Goes well with
- Artichoke, fennel and parmesan salad **p. 16**
- Herb salad with crushed hazelnuts **p. 18**

Pappardelle with walnuts, nutmeg and lemon

Sometimes only a big bowl of pasta will do, and this is a pasta dish that I make all year round. It bears some similarities to *cacio e pepe*, with a glossy, creamy sauce made from emulsifying cheese and butter with some of the pasta cooking water. The nutmeg brings a warmth that is very good with the nuttiness of roasted walnuts, then everything is enlivened with a zesty pep of lemon. In my opinion, this needs nothing more to accompany it other than good friends and perhaps some decent wine, but see the suggestions below if you fancy something fresh and green on the side.

Serves 4
Time 30 minutes

150g walnut halves or pieces
300g dried pappardelle
100g butter
¼ nutmeg
Sea salt and freshly cracked black pepper
200g Grana Padano or Parmesan (plus extra to serve)
Grated zest of 1 unwaxed lemon

Preheat the oven to 180°C fan. Arrange the walnuts in a single layer over a baking tray and roast for 10 minutes until they are lightly browned and smell nutty. Allow to cool, then roughly chop them and set aside.

Bring a large pan of salted water to the boil and cook the pappardelle according to the packet instructions. Before draining the pasta, scoop up a mug of the cooking water and set aside.

While the pasta is cooking, melt the butter in a wide, deep frying pan or saucepan. Grate in the nutmeg and crack in a generous amount of black pepper.

Drain the cooked pasta and transfer it to the pan, either pouring it from the colander or using tongs. Grate in the Grana Padano or Parmesan and add half of the reserved pasta cooking water. Stir to combine, allowing the cheese to melt. Slowly add more of the cooking water to achieve a glossy, creamy sauce.

Reserving some to garnish the finished dish, add most of the chopped walnuts along with the lemon zest. Toss until everything is well incorporated. Taste to check the seasoning, adjusting as needed.

Transfer the pappardelle to a large serving platter. Finish with some more finely grated Grana Padano or Parmesan, freshly cracked black pepper and the remaining chopped walnuts.

Do aheads
The walnuts can be roasted ahead of time.

Goes well with
- Artichoke, fennel and parmesan salad **p. 16**
- Chicory and pear seeded salad **p. 32**
- Winter greens with almonds and figs **p. 37**

Squash risotto with sage and pecan butter

When it comes to comfort food, risotto always wins. This comforting autumnal rice dish works so well as a cosy weeknight supper. The sage and pecan butter takes minutes to prepare but brings a glorious buttery indulgence that means it works beautifully when entertaining, too. I use onion squash as it has a delicious nuttiness and striking orange flesh. There is no need to peel away the skin either as, when roasted, the outer layer becomes buttery soft, melting beautifully into the risotto. If you cannot find an onion squash, a butternut squash will do. You will have leftover squash after roasting, but I tend to toss any leftovers into salads or even smoosh them on toast.

Serves 4–6
Time 1 hour 30 minutes

1 medium onion squash (or butternut squash)

Olive oil

Coarse sea salt flakes

1 large shallot or white onion, finely chopped

2 garlic cloves, finely chopped

250g arborio risotto rice

About ¼ of a fresh nutmeg

Large glass (250ml) of dry white wine

500–600ml hot vegetable or chicken stock

Good knob of butter

50g Grana Padano or Parmesan

For the sage and pecan butter

80g butter

30g pecans, roughly chopped

About 12 sage leaves

Preheat the oven to 200°C fan. Cut the squash in half, remove the seeds and cut into wedges. (If you like, rinse and pat dry the seeds before roasting them with olive oil and sea salt on a parchment paper-lined tray in an oven set to 180°C fan for 30 minutes for a crunchy snack.)

Place the squash wedges onto a roasting tray, drizzle with olive oil and generously season with sea salt. Roast for 40 minutes or until the squash is cooked through and slightly charred at the edges. Allow to cool slightly.

Keeping the skin on, place 300g of the squash wedges in a bowl and gently break up the flesh using a fork. If using butternut squash, remove and discard the skin and just use 300g of the cooked flesh.

Heat a good glug of olive oil in a large, heavy-based pan set over a low heat. Add the shallot or onion and cook for about 5 minutes or until softened. Add the garlic and cook for a further minute.

Stir the rice through the cooked shallot/onion and garlic, then grate the nutmeg into the pan. Allow it to cook for a few minutes then pour in the wine and cook, stirring, until the liquid has been absorbed.

Begin to slowly add the stock, one ladleful at a time, stirring occasionally. Only add more stock once the previous addition has been nearly absorbed. After 20 minutes, test the rice – it is ready when nearly cooked through but still with a little bite. You may not need to add all of the stock.

Once the rice has reached this stage, add the broken-up squash along with the butter. Give everything a good stir and cook for about 5 minutes until the risotto has taken on the colour of the squash. Grate in the Grana Padano or Parmesan and stir until well incorporated. Cover the pan with a lid, then switch off the heat while you make the sage and pecan butter.

Do aheads

The squash can be roasted hours ahead or even the day before, if you like to free up oven space.

Goes well with

- Winter greens with almonds and figs **p. 37**
- Chicory and pear seeded salad **p. 32**

Melt the butter in a small saucepan over a medium heat. Add the chopped pecans and sage leaves, then cook for a further 5 minutes or until the sage leaves are crisp and the butter has begun to deposit small dark flecks on the bottom of the pan. Switch off the heat.

Return to the risotto. Adjust the seasoning to taste. You may need to loosen it with a touch more stock. Spoon the risotto into bowls, then spoon over the pecan and sage butter.

Saffron butter beans

This is inspired by *risotto alla Milanese*, a simple yet incredibly elegant rice dish made with saffron. The method here is much the same, except I use butter beans in place of the rice. It is a comforting twist on this Italian classic that takes a fraction of the time to prepare. I often cook this for Friday night's supper when I fancy something that feels a little bit special but doesn't require much effort. Look for good-quality jarred butter beans for this, if you can, as their beany stock brings a wonderful creaminess to this. If you are cooking for more, it is simple to multiply.

Serves 2–4
Time 25 minutes

Good pinch of saffron
Olive oil
1 shallot, finely diced
700g jar of butter beans, including their liquid
20g butter, at room temperature, cubed
30g Grana Padano or Parmesan, finely grated

To serve
100g crème fraîche
Small handful of dill, chopped
Freshly cracked black pepper

Place 3 tablespoons of just-boiled water in a small ramekin or bowl. Add the saffron to the bowl, lightly crushing it between your fingers as you add it to the water. Allow to steep for 5 minutes.

Meanwhile, heat a good glug of olive oil in a large frying pan over a gentle heat. Add the diced shallot and cook for 5 minutes or until soft and translucent.

Pour the butter beans into the pan along with their liquid from the jar, the infused saffron water and the saffron strands. Stir to combine, then simmer for 5–7 minutes, stirring occasionally, until warmed through.

Stir in the butter and grated Grana Padano or Parmesan, then reduce the heat and cook gently for a further 2–3 minutes until the cheese has completely melted and you have a smooth, glossy sauce. Season to taste.

Spoon the beans into bowls, then top each portion with a spoonful of the crème fraîche and finish with some chopped dill and freshly cracked black pepper.

Goes well with
- Chicory and pear seeded salad **p. 32**
- Cavolo nero with anchovy, chilli and hazelnuts **p. 63**
- Bitter leaf salad with soft eggs **p. 38**

Red wine–braised lentils

Lentils don't get the attention they deserve in my opinion. Too often dismissed as being mushy or stodgy, they are frequently overlooked when it comes to deciding what to have for supper. These lentils are gently braised in red wine with lots of aromatics until they are soft yet maintain a good bite. I use glossy black beluga lentils as they retain their shape and al dente texture even when cooked for a long time. The salsa verde perks them up and brings a vibrancy to the whole thing. If you can't find beluga lentils, Puy lentils work well, too, but may require a little more liquid.

Serves 6
Time 1 hour 10 minutes

Olive oil
1 white onion or 2 large shallots, finely diced
1 small fennel bulb, trimmed and finely diced
2 carrots, finely diced
2 garlic cloves, finely grated
½ tsp chilli flakes
2 tbsp thyme leaves
500g dried black beluga or Puy lentils
300ml red wine
500ml stock (chicken or vegetable)
2 bay leaves
200g cavolo nero or kale, leaves torn or roughly chopped
Coarse sea salt flakes

To serve
Salsa verde (**p. 196**)

First, make the salsa verde (see page 196) to allow the flavours to settle. If you prefer this to be vegetarian, omit the anchovies. It is up to you whether you make a coarsely chopped or smooth blitzed salsa verde. I tend to prefer the latter for this dish, but both are delicious options.

Heat a glug of olive oil in a wide, deep frying pan over a low-medium heat. Add the diced onion or shallots, fennel and carrots, then gently cook for 8–10 minutes or until softened. Add the garlic, chilli flakes and thyme leaves (and any remaining anchovies left from making the salsa verde, if you like and don't need to keep it vegetarian) and cook for another couple of minutes.

Rinse and drain the lentils, then add them to the pan along with the red wine, stock and bay leaves. Season with a good pinch of sea salt flakes. Bring to the boil, then reduce to a gentle simmer, cover and cook for 30–40 minutes, stirring occasionally. The lentils should be almost cooked through but still with a little bite and almost all the liquid should have been absorbed. Fish out the bay leaves.

Add the cavolo nero or kale to the pan, stir it through the lentils, cover with a lid and cook for a further 5–10 minutes until wilted. Taste to check the seasoning, adjusting as needed.

Serve the braised lentils with the salsa verde either on the side or spooned over.

Do aheads
The salsa verde can be made a day ahead and kept refrigerated.

Goes well with
- Herb salad with crushed hazelnuts **p. 18**
- Chicory and pear seeded salad **p. 32**
- Za'atar cabbage, fennel, apple slaw **p. 40**

Fruit and nut rice

My mother is an excellent host and throws a summer party every year, for which she and I do all the cooking. We always serve a big wild rice salad, piled high onto a large platter for everyone to help themselves. Sometimes we add some griddled vegetables – courgettes and aubergines make nice additions – but the base is always red or wild rice, soft spring onions, citrus zest, chopped nuts and lots of fresh herbs. I make this rice dish ahead of time as I think this tastes best cold. I also tend to make more than I need and keep the leftovers in the fridge to eat across the next couple of days, but you can halve the quantities, if you wish. My top advice is to add the nuts and herbs just before serving to retain their texture. *Pictured on page 120.*

Serves 8–10
Time 1 hour 5 minutes

Olive oil
3 bunches of spring onions (about 300g), finely sliced
350g red Camargue rice or wild rice
Grated zest and juice of 1 orange
Grated zest and juice of 1 unwaxed lemon
2 tbsp sherry vinegar or red wine vinegar
1 garlic clove, finely grated
Sea salt
100g dried figs (or apricots), roughly chopped
100g pistachios, roughly chopped
100g roasted almonds or hazelnuts, roughly chopped
Large bunch of parsley (about 50g), roughly chopped
Small bunch of dill (about 25g), roughly chopped
Small bunch of mint (about 25g), roughly chopped

Heat a glug of olive oil in a deep saucepan with a lid set over a medium heat. Add the spring onions and cook for 5–6 minutes or until soft. Transfer to a plate and set aside.

Using the same saucepan, cook the rice according to the packet instructions.

In a small bowl, combine 5 tablespoons of olive oil with the citrus zests and juices, vinegar and grated garlic to make a dressing.

Once cooked, drain the rice and return it to the pan. Stir the dressing and a good pinch of salt into the rice, then add the softened spring onions and chopped figs. Cover the pan with the lid and allow the rice to stand for 10 minutes so the fruit softens.

Allow the rice to cool slightly if serving straight away or to cool fully if you intend to enjoy it cold. Just before serving, stir through the chopped nuts and herbs, then season to taste.

Do aheads

I will usually make it a day ahead, allowing the fruit and rice to plump up and take on the flavour of the dressing. If you can, add the nuts and herbs just before serving to keep their crunch. But any leftovers with nuts and herbs already added will taste very good kept in the fridge for a couple of days, too.

Goes well with
- Spiced aubergine on cold garlic yogurt **p. 71**
- Stuffed squid with tomatoes and feta **p. 144**
- Prawn saganaki **p. 52**

Brothy beans with cavolo nero and chicken

This is a riff on a classic Tuscan bean stew, but with added chicken. There is something incredibly soothing about making this, and while I would usually advise cooks to have all the ingredients ready before they begin, this is a recipe that lends itself very well to prepping as you go. A tip for preparing the cavolo nero is to pull the leaves starting at the thick stem end and pulling in one smooth action. You will be left with the rich green leaves, ready to be cooked, and the naked stems, which you can keep for stock. I tend to roast a chicken once a week and usually have some leftovers knocking about in my fridge. However, if you are cooking everything from scratch, I have included instructions for how to poach the chicken.

Serves 4

Time 35 minutes or 1 hour 10 minutes if poaching the chicken

1 large banana shallot or ½ white onion

1 fennel bulb, trimmed

1 carrot

Olive oil

1 fat garlic clove, peeled

1 tsp chilli flakes

1 tbsp thyme leaves

700g jar of cannellini or butter beans, including their liquid

1 litre stock (either vegetable or chicken stock, or the cooking liquid from poaching the chicken)

170g cavolo nero leaves, pulled from the stems and roughly chopped

2 good handfuls of shredded cooked chicken or 2 chicken breasts (see below)

Coarse sea salt flakes

To poach the chicken breasts

2 skinless chicken breasts

1 bay leaf

½ unwaxed lemon, sliced

1 carrot, roughly chopped

1 large shallot or ½ onion, halved

1 garlic clove, smashed with the flat of a knife

Few cavolo nero stems (optional)

If poaching the chicken breasts, do this first. Place the chicken in a saucepan with the bay leaf, sliced lemon, chopped carrot, onion and smashed garlic. Pour in enough water to submerge the chicken. Add a good pinch of salt. Bring the water to the boil, then lower to a simmer and cook the chicken over the lowest heat for 15 minutes or until the chicken juices run clear. Remove the chicken from the pan and allow it to rest for 10 minutes before tearing/shredding or slicing. I prefer to tear/shred it for this dish. Continue to simmer the poaching liquid for a further 10 minutes. Use this liquid as the stock for the beans, stirring through a crumbled stock cube, if you like.

Finely dice the shallot or onion, fennel and carrot – these will form the base of the *soffritto*. Heat a large glug of olive oil in a deep pan set over a low-medium heat. Add the chopped vegetables and gently cook for 8–10 minutes or until softened but not coloured. Finely grate in the garlic, then add the chilli flakes and thyme leaves. Cook for a further minute, then add the beans along with their liquid from the jar and the stock. Bring to a simmer and cook for 3–4 minutes.

Measure out three ladlefuls of the mixture from the pan, transfer to a blender (I use a Nutribullet) and blitz until smooth. Return to the pan.

Add the cavolo nero to the pan and simmer for 3 minutes until wilted. Scatter in the shredded chicken with a good pinch of flaky salt and simmer for a further 5 minutes until everything is piping hot. Taste to check the seasoning, adjusting if needed, and then serve.

Do aheads

I tend to roast a chicken once a week and have leftovers, but if you are poaching the chicken from scratch, you could do this the day before, too.

Goes well with

- Green beans with Pecorino and pine nuts p. 34
- Winter greens with almonds and figs p. 37

BAKED

HARISSA SESAME CARROTS
WITH LABNEH
95

CRISPY ZA'ATAR
SMASHED POTATOES
96

FILO BAKED FETA WITH
HARISSA AND HONEY
98

PEA, PANCETTA AND
PECORINO TART
100

BAKED RICOTTA WITH
ROMANO PEPPERS
102

CHICKEN WITH SAFFRON
AND CHICKPEAS
104

HAKE PUTTANESCA
105

FENNEL, SHALLOT,
TOMATO AND GARLIC
CONFIT WITH BURRATA
108

BAKED CHICKEN WITH
LA RATTE POTATOES
AND ROMESCO
111

GNUDI WITH ROASTED
TOMATO SAUCE
112

ONE-TRAY SPATCHCOCKED
CHICKEN WITH HERBY RICE
114

ROASTED BEETROOT WITH
WHIPPED FETA AND GREEN
CHILLI SALSA
116

BAKED LEEKS WITH
HAZELNUT CHILLI BUTTER
118

CRISPY CHICKEN
THIGHS WITH LEMON
AND PINK PEPPERCORNS
119

BAKED SALMON WITH
BLOOD ORANGE AND CHILLI
122

FENNEL, THYME AND CRÈME
FRAÎCHE GRATIN
124

CIDER-BRAISED CHICKEN
WITH APPLES
127

There is little as comforting as the thought of something bubbling away in the oven. The joy that a few ingredients can be combined together and left for 40 minutes, without the need for any prodding and poking, only to reappear as something entirely different and completely delicious is nothing short of magic in my opinion. When people ask me what to cook, I usually say a few good cold or room temperature bits and one 'bung-it-in-the-oven' dish. Something that you can forget about for a bit while losing yourself in good conversation, or perhaps a nice long bath. Years ago, I suspect half of these recipes would be traditionally considered as 'main courses' with the other half as sides, but I think most of us cook differently now, I certainly do. Whether you intend to enjoy them as the centrepiece to lunch with friends, or propped up on your knees on the sofa, they are best accompanied by something fresh. I've made suggestions for each but encourage you to flick through the TOSSED chapter for more ideas.

Harissa sesame carrots with labneh

I often get asked for showstopper dishes to make when cooking for vegetarians, and this is one that I pull out time and time again. Carrots love a bit of heat and harissa brings a complex almost fruity heat here. I am a spice fiend, so love to add a pinch of cayenne pepper, too. The sesame seeds give the carrots a crunchy coating with some of them catching the spicy stickiness in the pan almost like a savoury granola. Everything is drizzled with silky sweet honeyed tahini, with any crunchy seeds left in the pan sprinkled over to garnish. It's one that looks far more impressive than the sum of its parts and it tastes excellent the next day, too. Making labneh is incredibly easy, however, it needs a little forward planning as you have to start it at least 6 hours before you intend to eat. If you have not left enough time, just whisk the yogurt with some finely grated garlic and a pinch of salt and serve it as garlicky yogurt instead.

Serves 4–6

Time 40 minutes, plus overnight resting for the labneh

For the harissa sesame carrots

2 bunches of baby carrots or 1kg of carrots

5 tbsp olive oil

1 tbsp apple cider vinegar

1 tbsp runny honey

1 tbsp harissa paste

½ tsp cayenne pepper (optional)

2 tsp fennel seeds

30g sesame seeds

Pinch of coarse sea salt flakes

For the honeyed tahini

3 tbsp tahini

1 tbsp runny honey

To serve

Labneh **p. 190**

At least 6 hours ahead or ideally the day before, make the labneh following the instructions on page 190. Once the labneh has hung, discard the liquid. Give the labneh a quick stir to soften it slightly.

Preheat the oven to 200°C fan. Wash the carrots, then slice them in half lengthways, quartering any very large ones. Arrange the carrots in a single layer over a roasting tray. Mix the olive oil, apple cider vinegar, honey, harissa, cayenne pepper (if using), fennel seeds and sesame seeds in a small bowl. Season with the sea salt. Pour this sticky mixture over the carrots and, using your hands, toss until well coated. Roast the carrots for 25 minutes or until cooked and slightly charred.

For the honeyed tahini, mix the tahini and honey in a bowl with a splash of water. Slowly add more water until you have a drizzle consistency. Do not be alarmed if the mixture seizes at first, just continue to gradually add more water until it reaches a glossy, smooth appearance.

Spread the labneh over a serving platter, top with the roasted carrots and drizzle over the honeyed tahini. Sprinkle over any remaining crunchy sesame bits scraped up from the tray.

Do aheads

The labneh and honeyed tahini can both be made a day or two ahead. Keep in the fridge until an hour before serving. Add a little extra water to the tahini if it needs loosening.

Goes well with

- Red wine-braised lentils **p. 86**
- Fruit and nut rice **p. 87**
- Herby meatballs with green tahini **p. 60**

Crispy za'atar smashed potatoes

A crispy potato is a wonderful thing, but while I enjoy a classic roast potato, I sometimes find the process a bit of a chore. These smashed potatoes never let me down and require only minimal effort. The potatoes are parboiled before being tossed in olive oil and za'atar, then smashed with the base of a glass and cooked in the oven without any need for further poking or tossing. The skins are left on the potatoes for extra flavour. Cooking them this way means that the edges become gloriously crispy. Look for even-sized, slightly smaller potatoes, if you can; this ensures that all of them get a good level of crispiness.

Serves 4–6
Time 1 hour 15 minutes

For the smashed potatoes
800g new potatoes
Olive oil
1–2 tbsp za'atar
Sea salt

For the roasted garlic yogurt
2 whole bulbs of garlic
 (or 1 whole bulb of smoked garlic)
300g full-fat Greek yogurt
Good pinch of sea salt
Juice of ½ lemon

To serve
Salsa verde (**p. 196** – I recommend coarsely chopped)

Preheat the oven to 190°C fan. Slice the bases from the bulbs of garlic before wrapping them in foil. Roast the garlic for 30–40 minutes or until soft. Allow the garlic to cool, then squeeze out the flesh from the cloves and combine it in a food processor with 150g of the yogurt, a good pinch of sea salt and the lemon juice. Blitz until smooth. Fold into the remaining yogurt and chill until ready to serve.

Bring a large pan of salted water to the boil. Add the new potatoes and cook for 15–20 minutes or until you can easily pierce them with a knife. Drain the potatoes, then allow them to stand in a colander for a few minutes to steam dry.

Transfer the potatoes to a large baking dish, drizzle liberally with olive oil, then scatter over 1 tablespoon of the za'atar and a good pinch of sea salt. Give them a good toss to coat. Using the base of a glass, gently crush each potato. Sprinkle a little more za'atar over each potato, then roast for 30–40 minutes or until golden and crispy.

While the potatoes cook, make the salsa verde following the instructions on page 196.

Spoon the roasted garlic yogurt over a serving platter, pile on the smashed potatoes and spoon over the salsa verde, then serve.

Do aheads
- The garlicky yogurt can be made a day ahead and refrigerated.
- The salsa verde can be made up to a day ahead and kept in the fridge until 1 hour before serving.

Goes well with
- Pan-fried chicken with chilli, tomatoes and mint **p. 58**
- Harissa honey chicken wings **p. 151**
- Grilled bream with charred spring onion salsa **p. 147**

Filo baked feta with harissa and honey

I first tried a variation of this dish at a fabulous beach restaurant on a tiny Greek island called Lipsi. They served the filo-wrapped feta piping hot, drizzled with local honey and tahini. To this day, it remains one of the most delicious things I have ever eaten. I love the addition of rose harissa here, which adds a spicy, jammy element to the creamy feta as it bakes.

Serves 4
Time 35 minutes

1 heaped tbsp rose harissa paste (I use Belazu)
Olive oil
2 sheets of filo pastry
200g block of feta

To serve
1 tbsp tahini
1 tbsp runny honey
Generous pinch of toasted sesame seeds

Preheat the oven to 200°C fan.

Combine the rose harissa paste with 1 tablespoon of olive oil to loosen it.

Unroll the sheets of filo pastry. Using a pastry brush (or clean paint brush), coat one of the sheets of filo with olive oil.

Working from a narrow end of the filo, paint or spread half the harissa paste in the rough shape of the feta in the centre of the filo sheet, leaving a clear 3-cm border from the edge of the pastry. Place the feta on top of the filo and spread the remaining harissa paste over the cheese. Fold in the two short sides of the pastry, then brush the length of the filo with more olive oil. Next, fold the feta over onto itself to create a neatly wrapped parcel.

Brush the second sheet of filo with more olive oil, place the feta parcel in the centre of the pastry and repeat the folding and wrapping process once again.

Brush the filo-wrapped parcel with olive oil and transfer to a baking tray. Bake the feta for 20 minutes or until crisp and golden.

Using a spatula, carefully lift the feta onto a serving plate. Drizzle over the tahini and honey, then sprinkle on the toasted sesame seeds. Enjoy while warm.

Goes well with
- Tomato salad **p. 41**
- Carrot and coriander salad **p. 24**
- Agrodolce aubergines **p. 51**

Pea, pancetta and pecorino tart

A good savoury tart can wear many hats. I have enjoyed this one as part of a summer lunch with friends, as a weekend brunch or even from a plate balanced on my knees as a midweek tv supper. A generous dose of fresh herbs brings a springy note to this, and while you can find the ingredients all year round, I think it tastes best during spring and summer. I lean on frozen peas for the most part when making this as I always have them in my freezer, but if you can get hold of fresh peas, it is all the more delicious. I make my pastry in a food processor, which couldn't be simpler, but I have also included instructions for how to do this by hand. Homemade pastry makes all the difference and so it is well worth it, especially in this case where the pastry is studded with crunchy, aromatic fennel seeds. You can serve this tart warm or cool. I think it tastes best at room temperature, so I tend to make it ahead of time to allow the flavours to settle. Spelt flour lends a subtle nuttiness to the pastry, but regular flour works well, too.

Serves 10

Time 1 hour 30 minutes, plus chilling time

For the pastry

2 tsp fennel seeds

250g white spelt flour or plain white flour (plus extra for dusting)

Pinch of fine sea salt

140g cold unsalted butter, cubed

1 large egg, lightly beaten

1–2 tsp ice-cold water

For the filling

80g diced pancetta (I prefer unsmoked, but use smoked if you wish)

200g frozen peas, or 150g podded fresh

3 eggs

200ml double cream

1 fat garlic clove, finely grated or crushed

120g Pecorino, finely grated

Small bunch of chives (about 25g), finely chopped

Small bunch of tarragon (about 25g), leaves finely chopped

Small bunch of dill (about 25g), finely chopped

Good pinch of sea salt

You will also need a 22-cm loose-based, fluted tart tin.

In a dry frying pan set over a low heat, toast the fennel seeds for 1–2 minutes or until they begin to smell fragrant. Transfer to a plate and leave to cool.

Place the flour and salt in the bowl of your food processor and blitz to combine. Add the cold butter and blitz again until the mixture resembles breadcrumbs. Add the toasted fennel seeds and pulse just a few times to combine. Next, add the egg and 1 teaspoon of the ice-cold water, then pulse again until the mixture starts to come together as a pastry dough. Only add more water if needed.

To make the pastry by hand, whisk together the flour and salt in a large mixing bowl. Add the cold butter and rub it into the flour with your fingers until the mixture resembles breadcrumbs. Add the toasted fennel seeds and rub those in, too. Next, add the egg and 1 teaspoon of the ice-cold water, then bring the mixture together as a pastry dough with your hands, adding more water if needed.

Tip the pastry dough onto a lightly floured surface and shape it into a disc with your hands. Tightly wrap the dough in bees wax wrap or cling film and chill in the fridge for at least 1 hour.

While the pastry chills, fry the pancetta in a frying pan over a medium heat (there is no need to add any additional oil) for 3–5 minutes or until cooked and charred in places. Transfer the pancetta to a kitchen paper-lined plate to absorb any excess oil.

Blanch the frozen peas in boiling water for just 2 minutes (or 1½ minutes if using fresh). Immediately plunge them into ice-cold water until cool, then drain again.

Preheat the oven to 180°C fan.

Place the chilled pastry dough on a lightly floured surface and roll out to a thickness of 5-mm and about 30-cm round. Use the rolled-out pastry to line a 22-cm loose-based, fluted tart tin, allowing the excess pastry to overhang the sides of the tin. Trim the excess pastry to slightly higher than the edge of the tin (this is to allow for shrinkage when the pastry cooks). Line the pastry case with parchment paper and fill with ceramic baking beans, then bake blind in the hot oven for 20 minutes. Remove the baking beans and parchment paper, then return the pastry case to the oven and bake for a further 10 minutes until the pastry is dry. Set aside while you finish the filling.

In a large bowl, loosely beat the eggs with a whisk. Add the cream, garlic, Pecorino and chopped herbs, along with a good pinch of sea salt. Whisk again. Stir through the cooked pancetta and peas.

Carefully pour the filling mixture into the part-baked tart case and bake for 30–35 minutes or until golden with the edges set and the middle retaining a slight wobble. Do not be alarmed if the filling puffs slightly, it will relax as it cools. Leave the tart to settle for 10 minutes, then carefully remove from the tin and transfer to a plate or wire rack to cool before serving.

Do aheads
- The pastry can be made a day ahead and even rolled into the tart shell and left in the fridge until ready to bake.
- This tart also tastes very good the next day, so feel free to make the entire thing a day ahead. Keep it refrigerated overnight, then bring back to room temperature before serving.

Goes well with
- Herb salad with crushed hazelnuts **p. 18**
- Salsa verde salad **p. 25**
- Charred spring onions with burrata, peas and dill **p. 143**

Baked ricotta with romano peppers

I adore ricotta, so much so that I am never without at least two tubs in my fridge. There are various methods for baking ricotta, some more complicated than others. This is about as simple as it gets and merely requires you to plop it onto a tray and slot it into the oven. Rather than melt under the heat as, say, a Cheddar does, ricotta firms up, becoming richer and creamier. It is glorious simply spread onto some good bread and sprinkled with a little salt, but I also love it with the addition of sweet Romano peppers roasted alongside on the tray. Some people opt to remove the skins of Romano peppers after roasting, but I rather enjoy the texture they bring. Do not skimp on the sherry vinegar on the peppers. Rather than making them sharp it somehow manages to heighten their sweetness.

Serves 4–6
Time 45 minutes

4 Romano peppers
Olive oil
Sea salt
250g tub of ricotta
3 tbsp sherry, Moscatel or red wine vinegar
1 tbsp capers, rinsed and drained
Handful of finely chopped parsley
Good bread, to serve

Preheat the oven to 190°C fan.

Halve the Romano peppers lengthways, leaving their stems in place but scraping out the seeds. Place the peppers on a large roasting tray, drizzle liberally with olive oil, sprinkle with sea salt and toss to coat. Rearrange the peppers on the tray, skin side down.

Cut a round of parchment paper just slightly bigger than the ricotta. Place the paper disc on the roasting tray with the peppers, if space allows, or a separate baking tray, if it does not. Decant the ricotta onto the parchment paper – essentially, this means plop the ricotta from its tub onto the paper disc on the tray. Drizzle with olive oil and season with sea salt.

Bake the peppers and ricotta for 35–40 minutes or until the peppers are soft and the ricotta has taken on a little colour. Sprinkle the vinegar over the peppers while still warm.

Gently pick up the ricotta and transfer it to a round serving tray, then arrange the roasted peppers around it. Scatter over the capers and parsley, then serve.

Goes well with
- Artichoke, fennel and parmesan salad **p. 16**
- Queen Caesar salad **p. 23**
- Crispy za'atar smashed potatoes **p. 96**
- Charred spring onions with burrata, peas and dill **p. 143**

Chicken with saffron and chickpeas

This is what I fondly refer to as a 'bung-it-in-the-oven dish', however, the inclusion of beautifully potent saffron elevates it to something slightly more special. The whole thing is tossed together and cooked in one dish in about an hour. The chickpeas take the place of potatoes or rice, and there's more room (not to mention time) for a chorus of salads or other vegetable dishes on the table (see below for suggestions). I tend to give the chicken just a 30-minute marinate ahead of cooking, but if you want to get ahead, you can prepare the chicken earlier or even the night before and store it in the fridge.

Serves 4
Time 1 hour, plus 30 minutes marinating

Good pinch of saffron
2 tsp fennel seeds
100ml dry white wine
Juice of 1 lemon
4 garlic cloves, peeled and smashed with the flat of your knife
Olive oil
Sea salt
4 chicken legs, bone in and skin on
700g jar of chickpeas, drained
Small bunch of basil (about 25g)

Place 2 tablespoons of just-boiled water in a small ramekin or bowl. Add the saffron to the bowl, lightly crushing it between your fingers as you add it to the water. Allow to steep for 5 minutes.

Meanwhile, toast the fennel seeds in a dry frying pan set over a low heat until they smell fragrant, then leave to cool.

In a bowl large enough to hold all the chicken, combine the infused saffron water, toasted fennel seeds, white wine, lemon juice and garlic with a generous glug of olive oil and good pinch of sea salt. Add the chicken and toss to coat. Cut the juiced lemon into quarters and drop those in, too. Leave to marinate at room temperature for 30 minutes. If marinating ahead, refrigerate, then be sure to remove the chicken from the fridge at least 30 minutes before cooking, but no longer than 1 hour.

Preheat the oven to 190°C fan.

Pour the chickpeas into a large, ovenproof dish. Arrange the marinated chicken, skin side up, on top of the chickpeas and pour over the remaining marinade, making sure the garlic is evenly dispersed. Season the chicken skin with sea salt.

Cook the chicken and chickpeas in the oven for 45 minutes, by which time the chicken should be cooked through with crispy skin. Using tongs, momentarily move the chicken to side of the dish, tear in the basil and stir it through the chickpeas. Serve everyone directly from the dish, spooning a pile of chickpeas onto everyone's plate and perching the chicken on top, or spreading all the chickpeas over a serving platter and nestling the chicken in the pile.

Do aheads

You can marinate the chicken the day before, just be sure to remove the chicken from the fridge at least 30 minutes before cooking.

Goes well with

- Artichoke, fennel and parmesan salad **p. 16**
- Pan-fried courgettes with mozzarella and pistachio butter **p. 54**
- Salsa verde salad **p. 25**

Hake puttanesca

Puttanesca is king of the pasta sauces: saucy, punchy and full of flavour. There are many stories surrounding the origin of *spaghetti alla puttanesca*, but most accounts agree that the dish became popular in Naples due to the combination of ingredients being inexpensive, as well as being things most Neapolitans already had in their cupboard. This was a bit of a spur of the moment idea, based on what I had to hand. I made a classic puttanesca sauce, plonked the fish in the middle and baked it into what was a huge success. It is now a dish I have served to almost all of my friends. *Pictured overleaf.*

Serves 4
Time 1 hour

1 fennel bulb
200g cherry tomatoes
Olive oil
Sea salt
6 tinned anchovies, roughly chopped
4 garlic cloves, smashed and roughly chopped
1 tsp Aleppo pepper flakes
400g tin of chopped tomatoes
100ml white wine
2 tbsp red wine vinegar
2 tsp sugar
100g pitted Taggiasche or Kalamata olives
2 tbsp capers, drained and rinsed
6 thyme sprigs (plus extra to garnish)
500g hake (or other firm white fish), skin removed, cut into 4 even-sized pieces
Handful of chopped parsley (optional)

Preheat the oven to 200°C fan.

Trim the fennel bulb, reserving the fronds to use later as a garnish, if you like. Cut the fennel into thin wedges and arrange in a large, deep ovenproof dish. Pierce each tomato with a knife and add them to the dish with the fennel. Drizzle over about 1 tablespoon of olive oil and toss to coat. Season with a good pinch of sea salt.

Bake the fennel and tomatoes for 20 minutes. The fennel and tomatoes should be part-cooked with the tomatoes beginning to soften and the fennel browning in places.

Meanwhile, in a large saucepan, heat 3 tablespoons of olive oil over a low heat. Add the anchovies, garlic and Aleppo pepper flakes and cook until the anchovies have melted. Add the chopped tomatoes, wine, vinegar, sugar, olives, capers and thyme. Bring to the boil, then reduce to a simmer and cook, stirring occasionally, for 15 minutes until the sauce has reduced slightly.

Pour the puttanesca sauce from the pan over the fennel and tomatoes in the dish and give everything a bit of a stir. Nestle the hake pieces into the sauce, drizzle with more olive oil and sprinkle over some sea salt and a little extra thyme.

Return the dish to the oven and cook for 15–20 minutes or until the hake has cooked through. The fish should be opaque and should flake easily when teased with a knife.

Tear over any reserved fennel fronds or some chopped parsley, if you like.

Do aheads

The puttanesca sauce can be made up to a day ahead. It'll sit at room temperature for a few hours but put it in the fridge if you're keeping it overnight.

Goes well with

- Green beans with Pecorino and pine nuts (also pictured overleaf) **p. 34**
- Winter greens with almonds and figs **p. 37**
- New potatoes with anchovy chive butter **p. 77**

Fennel, shallot, tomato and garlic confit with burrata

Peeling two entire bulbs of garlic is a labour of love, but it is well worth it for this. The vegetables cook low and slow, becoming beautifully soft and jammy while infusing tonnes of flavour into the oil, which is excellent for dipping bread or dressing salads. I will often make a batch of the confit veg and return to it throughout the week, piling a heaped spoonful onto a piece of toast as a lazy summer lunch. But it is a brilliant dish for sharing, too. Burrata makes this particularly indulgent, but some torn mozzarella or heaped spoonfuls of ricotta work equally well.

Serves 4–6
Time 1 hour 20 minutes

- 4 banana shallots
- 2 fennel bulbs
- 400g baby plum tomatoes on the vine
- 2 whole bulbs of garlic, cloves peeled
- 3 large red chillies, halved lengthways (optional, omit if you don't like heat)
- Handful of rosemary sprigs
- Olive oil
- Sea salt
- 2 x 150g blobs of burrata
- Wholegrain focaccia (**p. 202**), to serve

Preheat the oven to 160°C fan.

Peel and halve the shallots lengthways.

Remove the tough outer layer from the fennel bulbs, trim the base and any woody bits, then cut lengthways into quarters or wedges. (Keep the trimmings for making a stock.)

Arrange the tomatoes, shallots, fennel, garlic and chillies (if using) in a deep, ovenproof dish, then scatter over the rosemary sprigs.

Pour over enough olive oil to almost cover the vegetables, filling the dish almost two-thirds full. Season generously with sea salt.

Bake the vegetables for about an hour or until the tomatoes, fennel and garlic are soft. Allow to cool slightly.

First, lift the rosemary from the oil and allow to drain on a kitchen paper-lined plate. Next, transfer the vegetables to a large serving platter, allowing some of the oil to come with them. Place the blobs of burrata alongside either on the same or a separate plate, tearing them open, if you like.

The drained, crispy rosemary leaves should now easily snap from their stems. Scatter the leaves over the vegetables and burrata to finish. I love to serve this dish with some bubbly focaccia for mopping up the oil.

Goes well with
- Asparagus and green bean mimosa salad **p. 15**
- Artichoke, fennel and parmesan salad **p. 16**
- Wholegrain focaccia (also pictured opposite) **p. 202**

Baked chicken with La Ratte potatoes and romesco

Usually, I am not hugely fussed about substitutions in recipes. I am of the camp that if you do not have coriander, you can just use parsley, or that if you do not like anchovies, you can simply leave them out. However, in this case, I must insist that you use La Ratte potatoes. They are longer and thinner than regular baby potatoes with a wonderfully waxy texture. When roasted, they hold their shape with their flavour becoming nuttier and buttery. You can find them in most big supermarkets and in all good greengrocers. This recipe is essentially a spin on chicken and chips but with a big spoonful of Spanish influence by way of romesco – a creamy, smoky red pepper sauce. I love to pile everything up onto the biggest serving dish I can find for everyone to help themselves at the table.

Serves 4–6
Time 1 hour 20 minutes

700g La Ratte potatoes, halved or quartered (depending on size)
Olive oil
Sea salt
2 banana shallots, quartered
6 skin-on, bone-in chicken thighs
2 tbsp thyme leaves
150ml white wine

For the romesco
175g blanched almonds
350g drained, jarred roasted red peppers
1 garlic clove, peeled and roughly chopped
2 tbsp sherry vinegar
1 tsp smoked paprika
1 tbsp olive oil
Good pinch of sea salt

Preheat the oven to 170°C fan.

First, toast the almonds for the romesco. Arrange the almonds in a single layer over a baking tray. Roast the almonds for 10 minutes or until golden brown. Allow them to cool.

Increase the oven temperature to 200°C fan.

Add the potatoes to a large roasting tray. Drizzle over a good glug of olive oil and season with a generous pinch of sea salt. Toss to coat. Roast the potatoes for 20 minutes or until beginning to brown. (This is when the potatoes gain most of their colour, so if some look a little pale, leave them to roast for a little longer.)

In a large bowl, toss the shallots and chicken with the thyme leaves, another glug of olive oil and a good pinch of sea salt. Add to the roasting tray with the potatoes, arranging the chicken skin side up, then pour over the wine ensuring you don't splash the chicken.

Season the chicken skin with a little more salt. Roast everything for 30–35 minutes or until the shallots are soft and the chicken skin is crispy. If your chicken skin has not browned enough, switch the oven to the grill setting for the last 5 minutes of the cooking time.

Meanwhile, make the romesco. Ensure the drained jarred peppers are dry by patting them with kitchen paper. Place the peppers in the bowl of a food processor along with half of the roasted almonds, the garlic, sherry vinegar, smoked paprika, olive oil and sea salt. Blitz together until smooth. Add the remaining almonds and pulse until the nuts have broken down but keep a bit of texture.

Transfer the chicken and potatoes to a large serving plate, and serve with the romesco alongside.

Do aheads
The romesco can be made up to 2 days ahead of time and kept in the fridge. Be sure to remove it from the fridge at least 30 minutes before serving so that it is at room temperature.

Goes well with
- Green beans with Pecorino and pine nuts **p. 34**
- Winter greens with almonds and figs **p. 37**
- Charred artichokes on minty yogurt **p. 47**

Gnudi with roasted tomato sauce

Gnudi take their name from the Italian word *nudi*, meaning naked. These pillowy soft balls are similar to what one might use as the filling for ravioli – only they are without the pasta shell and, therefore, naked. Here they are cooked in a rich, garlicky tomato sauce made simply by roasting tomatoes until they collapse into a sticky sauce. The one-tray nature of this dish means that the roasting tray gets quite a long stint in the oven. I like to line the tray with parchment paper as the tomatoes spit and splatter as they roast, which means they can leave char marks over the base. It also makes for less washing up which suits me well.

Serves 4–6
Time 1 hour 50 minutes

For the tomato sauce

1.5kg mixed tomatoes in different sizes and colours (San Marzano are lovely here)

6 fat garlic cloves, peeled but left whole

1 tsp chilli flakes

1 tsp thyme leaves

Olive oil

Sea salt

For the gnudi

250g ricotta

200g fresh spinach leaves

Bunch of tarragon or basil (about 25g), leaves picked

50g Grana Padano or Parmesan, finely grated (plus extra to serve)

Grated zest of 1 unwaxed lemon

1 large egg

Sea salt and freshly ground black pepper

30g plain flour

To serve

Salsa verde (**p. 196** – I recommend coarsely chopped)

Before making the gnudi, place the ricotta in a sieve set over a bowl and leave it for 30–40 minutes to allow any excess water to drain.

Meanwhile, preheat the oven to 200°C fan. Line a large, deep roasting tray with parchment paper.

Prepare the tomato sauce. Roughly chop the tomatoes and add them to the lined roasting tray, along with the garlic, chilli flakes and thyme. Drizzle over a generous glug of olive oil and season with a good pinch of sea salt. Toss to coat. Roast the tomatoes for about 1 hour, checking halfway through the cooking time and giving everything a bit of a stir. The tomatoes should collapse in on themselves, be sticky and charred in places with just a little of their liquid left. (The rest of the liquid will cook off once you add the gnudi.) Smoosh the garlic into the tomatoes and give the sauce a good stir. Taste to check the seasoning and adjust as needed.

As the tomatoes cook, prepare the gnudi. Add the spinach to a large saucepan with a good splash of water. Cover with a lid and cook over a medium heat until the spinach leaves wilt, stirring occasionally. Drain the spinach and allow it to cool before squeezing out as much moisture as you can. Be thorough with this or you will end up with soggy gnudi. Chop the spinach as finely as possible.

Finely chop the tarragon or basil leaves.

Place the chopped spinach and herbs in a bowl with the drained ricotta, grated Grana Padano or Parmesan, lemon zest and egg. Season well with salt and pepper. Stir together with a spoon until everything is well incorporated.

Once the roasted tomatoes are ready, gently fold the flour into the gnudi mixture. Scoop up a golf ball-sized dollop of the gnudi mixture and shape it into an oval (I use two tablespoons for this). Sit the gnudi in the tomato sauce in the roasting tray. Repeat with the remaining gnudi mixture, arranging them evenly over the tomato sauce. Return the tray to the oven for 25 minutes or until the gnudi are lightly browned.

Do aheads

The tomato sauce can be made a few hours ahead and kept at room temperature.

Goes well with

- Courgette, anchovy and lemon fritti p. 57
- Salsa verde salad p. 25
- Green beans with Pecorino and pine nuts p. 34

While the gnudi are baking, make the salsa verde following the instructions on page 196.

When ready to serve, drizzle the salsa verde over the cooked gnudi and serve straight from the roasting tray with any leftover salsa verde in a bowl on the side for people to add themselves.

One-tray spatchcocked chicken with herby rice

Do not be fooled by the simplicity of the recipe name. This is a one-tray dish with big flavour. The fennel gets a head start in the oven to gain a bit of colour before everything else goes in. As the chicken cooks on top of the rice, its gorgeous fatty juices trickle down, infusing flavour into the rice as the skin crisps up on top. It does require you peeling a whole bulb's worth of garlic cloves, but trust me, when it is jammy and golden and you are smooshing it into your rice, you will wish there was even more. As the chicken rests, the rice is stirred through with lots of fresh herbs and any crispy bits of rice that have caramelised around the edges of the roasting tray.

Serves 4–6
Time 1 hour 50 minutes

1 large chicken (approx. 1.75kg), spatchcocked
2 fennel bulbs
Olive oil
Salt and freshly ground black pepper
1 unwaxed lemon
1 whole bulb of garlic, cloves peeled
300g brown basmati rice
800ml chicken or vegetable stock
200ml dry white wine
Large bunch of dill (about 25g)
Bunch of mint (about 25g), leaves finely chopped
Large bunch of parsley (about 50g), leaves finely chopped
Small bunch of basil (about 25g), leaves left whole

Do aheads
The garlic cloves can be peeled up to a day ahead, and kept covered in the fridge.

Goes well with
- Salsa verde salad p. 25
- Artichoke, fennel and parmesan salad p. 16
- Herb salad with crushed hazelnuts p. 18

Remove the chicken from the fridge at least 30 minutes before cooking. Preheat the oven to 200°C fan.

Remove the tough outer layer from the fennel bulbs, trim the base and any woody bits. Roughly slice into 1-cm slices.

Place the fennel slices in a deep roasting tray that is large enough to hold the rice and chicken. Drizzle with olive oil, then season with salt. Cook the fennel in the oven for 15 minutes.

Meanwhile, using a serrated knife, work around the lemon, peeling away the rind and pith into thick strips roughly 2-cm wide.

Once the fennel has been cooking for 15 minutes, add the peeled garlic cloves, lemon rind and brown basmati rice to the roasting tray. Pour in the stock and wine, then give everything a good stir.

Drizzle the chicken with olive oil and rub it into the skin. Season with salt. Rest the chicken on top of the rice, adding more salt to the skin. Cover the tray with foil and cook for 1 hour.

After 1 hour, remove the foil and cook the chicken for a further 25 minutes. If you prefer the skin a little crispier, switch the oven to the grill setting for the last 5 minutes of the cooking time.

While the chicken finishes cooking, finely chop the dill, mint and parsley. I leave the basil leaves whole and allow them to wilt in, as spinach leaves would. They will lose some of their colour but none of their flavour.

Remove the chicken from the roasting tray and place on a board to rest for 10–15 minutes. Add all the fresh herbs to the tray with the rice, add a good glug of olive oil and squeeze in the juice of the lemon. Give everything a good stir until all the herbs have incorporated into the rice and the basil has started to wilt. Scrape up all the bits of crispy rice from the edges of the tray. Taste to check the seasoning, adjusting as needed.

Carve the chicken on the board and transfer the meat to a serving plate. Transfer the rice to a serving bowl. Or just serve up from the kitchen.

Roasted beetroot with whipped feta and green chilli salsa

Beetroot can be a bit of a Marmite vegetable. People either love it or they hate it. I love it, but I prefer fresh beetroot over ready-cooked and vacuum-packed, where I often find there is too much vinegar. The best way to cook beetroot is either to bake it whole or cook it like this, sliced thinly and roasted until lightly caramelised. The earthiness mellows into more of a sweetness as it roasts. It is the perfect match for tangy whipped feta and a herby green chilli salsa, both of which can be prepared ahead of time. I love to use a mix of candy beetroot and regular beetroot for this as the colours are so wonderful, but it is delicious made solely with regular beetroot, too.

Serves 4–6
Time 55 minutes

For the roasted beetroot

1kg beetroot (I love a mix of regular and candy beetroot for this)
1 tsp caraway seeds
1 tsp cumin seeds
Olive oil
Sea salt
Whipped feta (**p. 192**)

For the green chilli salsa

½ tsp cumin seeds
½ tsp caraway seeds
3 green chillies, deseeded and finely chopped (or you can leave the seeds in, if you like heat)
Small bunch of parsley (about 25g), finely chopped
Small bunch of mint (about 25g), finely chopped
1 garlic clove, crushed or finely grated
Juice of ½–1 lime
Olive oil

Preheat the oven to 190°C fan.

Wash, scrub and dry the beetroots before roughly slicing into 5-mm rounds, then toss with the caraway and cumin seeds, a good slosh of olive oil and a pinch of sea salt. Spread the beetroot slices over two roasting trays.

Roast the beetroot for 25–30 minutes, rotating the trays halfway through the cooking time. The beetroot should be soft and charred in places once it's ready.

Meanwhile, prepare the whipped feta following the recipe on page 192.

For the salsa, lightly toast the caraway and cumin seeds in a dry frying pan over a gentle heat until they begin to smell fragrant. Allow to cool, then combine with all the remaining ingredients for the salsa in a bowl, drizzling in enough olive oil to achieve a spoonable consistency.

When ready to serve, spoon the whipped feta onto a serving platter, top with the roasted beetroot slices and then spoon over the green chilli salsa.

Do aheads

Both the whipped feta and green chilli salsa can be made up to a day ahead and kept separately in the fridge.

Goes well with

- Grilled aubergines with green tahini **p. 134**
- Harissa honey chicken wings **p. 151**

Baked leeks with hazelnut chilli butter

These leeks are buttery soft with caramelised edges. Adding a little water to the roasting tray means that the leeks almost braise while gaining a good bit of colour. I think these are just as good at room temperature as they are warm from the oven, so I often make them ahead of time and then prepare the butter just before serving. Aleppo pepper flakes work deliciously here; if you cannot get hold of them, regular crushed chilli flakes work, too.

Serves 4–6
Time 45 minutes

6 medium–large leeks
Olive oil
Sea salt

For the hazelnut chilli butter

70g butter
20g roasted hazelnuts, chopped
½ tsp Aleppo pepper flakes (or use a pinch of crushed chilli flakes)
1 garlic clove, finely grated
Juice of ½ lemon or lime

Preheat the oven to 200°C fan.

Trim the green tops from the leeks, rinse away any dirt and pat dry with a clean tea towel. Halve the leeks widthways and then again lengthways. Arrange the leeks on a baking tray, drizzle generously with olive oil and sprinkle over some sea salt. Using your hands, make sure the leeks are well coated and each piece is seasoned.

Pour half a mugful of water directly onto the baking tray. (Do not worry about splashing the leeks; the water is to help them steam.) Bake the leeks for 30 minutes or until all the water has evaporated and the leeks are soft and golden.

Melt the butter over a medium heat in a small saucepan with the hazelnuts. Cook until the butter is frothing and the hazelnuts have turned golden, then switch off the heat. Stir through the Aleppo pepper flakes, garlic and lemon or lime juice along with a good pinch of sea salt. Allow the butter to rest for a couple of minutes.

Arrange the baked leeks on a large serving dish and spoon over the chilli hazelnut butter.

Do aheads
You can cook the leeks ahead of time and reheat before serving.

Goes well with
- Chicken with saffron and chickpeas **p. 104**
- Baked salmon with blood orange and chilli **p. 122**
- Pan-fried chicken with chilli, tomatoes and mint **p. 58**

Crispy chicken thighs with lemon and pink peppercorns

I have a lot of love for a one-tray supper, and it was this particular one-tray meal that sparked the idea for this book. It is a recipe that I cook repeatedly both for my family and when friends come round. It looks and tastes impressive but actually couldn't be simpler. As the chicken cooks, its juices trickle over the vegetables beneath, while in turn the vegetables have a steaming effect on the chicken, ensuring that the meat does not dry out. Meanwhile, the chicken skin crisps up on top. The end result is a perfectly juicy chicken with golden crispy skin and buttery soft, flavourful vegetables. It is important to use skin-on, bone-in chicken thighs for this, as they are by far the most flavoursome part of the bird. *Pictured overleaf.*

Serves 4–6
Time 55 minutes

4 banana shallots
2 fennel bulbs
1 unwaxed lemon
6–8 skin-on, bone-in chicken thighs
Small bunch of sage (about 25g), leaves picked
2 tbsp dried oregano
3 tbsp pink peppercorns (plus a few extra)
Olive oil
Sea salt
300ml dry white wine

Preheat the oven to 200°C fan.

Peel and quarter the shallots lengthways.

Remove the tough outer layer from the fennel bulbs, trim the base and any woody bits. (Keep the trimmings for making a stock.) Roughly slice the fennel into 2-cm wedges.

Halve the lemon lengthways, then cut each half into three wedges.

Arrange the shallots, fennel, lemon and chicken thighs in a large roasting tray. Add the sage leaves, dried oregano and pink peppercorns, crushing them slightly with your hands as you drop them in. Add a good glug of olive oil (about 6 tablespoons) along with a generous pinch of sea salt. Toss everything together. Rearrange the chicken thighs in the tray, sitting them on top of the vegetables with their skin side up.

Pour the wine into the tray, aiming it into the corners to avoid splashing the chicken. Drizzle some extra olive oil over the chicken thighs and season each one with a little more sea salt and a few more pink peppercorns (crushing them slightly in your hand).

Roast for 40 minutes until the chicken is cooked through with golden crispy skin. Check it after 35 minutes and if the skin has not browned enough, switch the oven to the grill setting for the last 5 minutes. Allow the chicken to rest for 5–10 minutes, then serve either directly onto plates with a good spoonful of the soft vegetables or arrange everything onto a platter. Finish by spooning over some of the citrusy juices from the pan.

Goes well with
- Fruit and nut rice (also pictured overleaf) **p. 87**
- Herb salad with crushed hazelnuts (also pictured overleaf) **p. 18**
- Grilled aubergines with green tahini **p. 134**
- Grilled cabbage with honey lime butter **p. 140**

Baked salmon with blood orange and chilli

I love cooking fish when people come over. It feels slightly elevated and special, but is usually very simple and takes a lot less time to cook than meat, meaning that if someone is late or the cocktails and conversation have run on, you don't have to wait an hour to eat. The colour of this salmon dish is fantastic and looks wonderful on the table – the blood oranges and Aleppo pepper flakes marry in the oven to create a vibrant sunset-red oil. I have suggested using salmon here, but it is very good with trout, too, which tends to be a more sustainable fish choice.

Serves 4
Time 35 minutes

1 tsp coriander seeds
2 blood oranges
3 fat garlic cloves
1–2 red chillies
600g salmon fillet, skin-on
5 tbsp olive oil
2 tsp Aleppo pepper flakes
Pinch of coarse sea salt flakes
Coriander leaves, to garnish

Preheat the oven to 200°C fan.

In a dry frying pan set over a low heat, toast the coriander seeds for 3–4 minutes or until they begin to smell fragrant. Transfer to a pestle and mortar and gently crush. (You can also use a small bowl and the base of a spice jar or end of a rolling pin for this.)

Thinly slice just one of the blood oranges, leaving the other one whole. Peel and thinly slice the garlic cloves. Halve the chillies lengthways, remove their seeds and cut them into thin matchsticks.

Put the salmon fillet in a large, ovenproof dish. Drizzle over the olive oil, then add the crushed coriander seeds, blood orange slices, garlic slices, red chilli matchsticks and Aleppo pepper flakes. Add the grated zest and juice of the remaining blood orange, then season with a good pinch of sea salt. Toss everything together, turning the salmon over a couple of times to ensure it is well coated in the marinade.

Lay the salmon fillet so it's skin side down and loosely arrange some of the blood orange slices and red chilli matchsticks on top. Bake the salmon for 15 minutes, then allow it to rest for a further 5 minutes. (The fish will continue to cook after it comes out of the oven.)

Just before serving, garnish the salmon with some coriander leaves.

Goes well with
- Herb salad with crushed hazelnuts (also pictured opposite) **p. 18**
- Fruit and nut rice **p. 87**
- Crispy za'atar smashed potatoes **p. 96**

Fennel, thyme and crème fraîche gratin

The first time I cooked this fennel gratin for me and my husband, the intention was to enjoy some of it alongside a roast chicken and save the rest for later. Somewhere between clearing the table and ferrying everything to the dishwasher, we found ourselves standing over the hob, each of us with a spoon and suddenly it was gone. I have made the same dish many times since, but tweaking it until I settled on this version where the fennel and onions are first cooked slowly on the hob until soft, and then baked in the oven with some nutmeg-spiked crème fraîche and a smattering of grated cheese. It does add an additional step outside of simply being baked in the oven, but it is one that is so worth it and you can do it well ahead of time if you need to free up hob space. This has a creamy, almost self-saucing element to it, which acts almost as a saucy condiment to whatever you pair it with. I can also confirm that leftovers (should there be any) are very good eaten on toast.

Serves 4–6

Time 1 hour 5 minutes (the first 30 minutes can be done ahead, leaving 20 minutes in the oven)

- 5 fennel bulbs
- 1 white onion
- 1 tbsp thyme leaves (plus extra to garnish)
- Olive oil
- Sea salt and freshly cracked black pepper
- 200g crème fraîche
- 100ml chicken or vegetable stock (or ½ stock cube dissolved in 100ml hot water)
- 1–2 pinches of finely grated nutmeg
- 50g finely grated Grana Padano or Parmesan

Remove the tough outer layer from the fennel bulbs, trim the base and any woody bits. (Keep the trimmings for making a stock.) Thinly slice the fennel – you can use a mandolin for this, if you have one.

Peel and thinly slice the onion.

Add the sliced fennel, onion and thyme to a deep pan, for which you have a lid. Drizzle over a good glug of olive oil, add a pinch of sea salt, then toss to coat. Place the dish over a low heat, cover with the lid and sweat down the fennel and onion for 30 minutes, stirring occasionally.

Preheat the oven to 180°C fan.

In a jug, mix together the crème fraîche, stock and grated nutmeg with a good pinch of sea salt and freshly cracked black pepper.

Once the fennel and onion have sweated down, transfer everything to an ovenproof dish roughly 20cm x 15cm. Pour over the crème fraîche mixture, then top with the grated Grana Padano or Parmesan and some extra thyme leaves.

Bake the gratin for 20 minutes or until browned and crispy on top. I like to pop the grill on for the last 5 minutes of the cooking time to make it really crispy. Serve straight away.

Do aheads

The fennel and onion can be cooked down on the hob up to 3 hours before and then kept at room temperature. You could also do it the day before and keep them in the fridge, just let them come back to room temperature before continuing.

Goes well with

- Pan-fried chicken with chilli, tomatoes and mint **p. 58**
- Pan-fried seabass with olive salsa **p. 64**
- Crispy chicken thighs with lemon and pink peppercorns **p. 119**

Cider–braised chicken with apples

I love this sort of hands-off cooking, especially in winter. After a bit of counter prep, once the chicken goes in the oven, you can forget about it for an entire hour. The chicken is seared first and, although an additional step, this brings so much flavour that you would be foolish not to do it. The end result is soft, tender meat that falls off the bone with a rich sauce that thickens into an almost glossy gravy as it cooks. I love to serve this with some waxy new potatoes boiled in well-salted water until soft, then drained and roughly broken up in the pan before being smothered in a generous pat of salted butter.

Serves 4–6
**Time 35 minutes hands-on,
1 hour 35 minutes in the oven**

- 80g smoked pancetta lardons
- 6–8 skin-on, bone-in chicken thighs
- 2 tbsp plain flour
- Sea salt and freshly ground black pepper
- 1 fennel bulb, trimmed and finely diced
- 2 shallots, finely diced
- 1 carrot, finely diced
- 3 garlic cloves, crushed
- 1 tbsp thyme leaves
- 1 large eating apple (I use Red Windsor), peeled, cored and roughly cut into 3-cm chunks
- 750ml cider
- 100g cavolo nero, stems removed and leaves roughly cut into 1-cm strips
- 2 bay leaves

Preheat the oven to 150°C fan.

In a large, deep casserole pot with a lid, cook the pancetta over a medium-high heat until crisp. Transfer the pancetta to a plate, leaving any fat in the pot.

Place the chicken thighs in a bowl or strong plastic bag along with the flour and a good pinch each of salt and black pepper. Toss or shake to evenly coat the chicken. Add the chicken thighs to the casserole pot with the pancetta fat and cook over a medium heat for a few minutes on each side to seal the meat and add some colour to the skin. Transfer the chicken to the plate with the pancetta.

Add the finely diced fennel, shallots and carrot to the same pot and gently cook for about 7 minutes or until soft. Scrape the base of the pot with a wooden spoon to allow the vegetables to pick up as much of the flavour from the pancetta and chicken as possible.

Add the garlic and thyme leaves to the pot and cook for another minute or so. Toss in the chopped apple and stir to coat, then pour in the cider and deglaze the pot.

Return the pancetta and chicken thighs to the casserole pot, then add the cavolo nero and bay leaves. Using tongs, rearrange the chicken thighs so that they are sat on top with the skin sides up. Bring everything to a simmer on the hob, then cover with a lid and transfer to the oven.

Cook the chicken for 1 hour 15 minutes, by which point the meat should be tender and almost falling off the bone. Remove the lid from the casserole pot, increase the oven temperature to 180°C fan and cook for a further 15–20 minutes or until browned, then serve.

Goes well with
- New potatoes with anchovy chive butter **p. 77**
- Chicory and pear seeded salad **p. 32**

GRILLED

GRILLED SUGAR SNAP PEAS
WITH LEMONY RICOTTA
133

GRILLED AUBERGINES
WITH GREEN TAHINI
134

CHARRED LETTUCE,
TWO WAYS
137

GRILLED CABBAGE WITH
HONEY LIME BUTTER
140

CHARRED SPRING ONIONS
WITH BURRATA, PEAS
AND DILL
143

STUFFED SQUID WITH
TOMATOES AND FETA
144

BUTTERFLIED LEG OF LAMB
WITH RED WINE VINEGAR
146

GRILLED BREAM WITH
CHARRED SPRING
ONION SALSA
147

HARISSA HONEY
CHICKEN WINGS
151

If I could, I think I would barbecue my food all year long. I love the slightly smoky char that cooking food this way brings. As it stands, I live in a country that rains approximately 100 days of the year and threatens to on at least 50 of the rest. And so, my barbecue sits patiently under its cover for the most part, waiting for the forecast to promise sun. I love the *dolce vita* feeling of cooking and eating outside, and if the sun is shining you can bet I will be dragging the table outside. But over the years, I've learnt that there are ways one can mimic that slightly charred, fiery taste and bring the feeling of easy holiday breeze to the kitchen at home. If you don't have a barbecue, or if the weather has rained on your parade (literally), for the recipes in this chapter, I have also included instructions for your oven or hob, which will do just as well.

Grilled sugar snap peas with lemony ricotta

It is often the simplest ingredient combinations that turn out to be the best. Such is the case with these peas. I love the sweet crunch of a sugar snap pea, especially when dipped into a silky mayonnaise or salty butter. These are a very slightly elevated version with the peas having a quick toss and turn on a hot grill. They sit somewhere between a snack and a sharing side – I often make them as part of a medley of good sharing bits with some nice bread for scooping up the last of the ricotta. The key is to make sure your griddle pan is very hot as you want the peas to char quickly rather than steam, so that they retain some bite. I love the simplicity of ricotta whipped with garlic and lemon as an accompaniment, but a homemade mayonnaise would also be lovely. I've shared a recipe on page 194.

Serves 4–6
Time 15 minutes

250g tub of ricotta
½ garlic clove, finely grated
Coarse sea salt
1 unwaxed lemon
400g sugar snap peas
Olive oil

Combine the ricotta, garlic and some sea salt in a bowl. Grate in most of the zest of the lemon, reserving some for serving. Set aside.

Toss the sugar snap peas in a glug of olive oil and a good pinch of sea salt.

Heat a griddle pan over a high heat until hot, then cook the peas in a single layer for about 3–4 minutes on each side until they have black char marks. You may need to work in two batches. Cut the zested lemon in half and add it to the griddle pan, cut side down, then cook it for a couple of minutes until it gains some colour.

Spread the lemon ricotta onto a serving plate, then top with the sugar snaps and the charred lemon halves for squeezing over. Finish with the reserved lemon zest.

Do aheads
The ricotta mixture can be combined a couple of hours ahead and kept in the fridge until serving.

Goes well with
- Agrodolce aubergines **p. 51**
- Pan-fried chicken with chilli, tomatoes and mint **p. 58**
- Pea, pancetta and pecorino tart **p. 100**

Grilled aubergines with green tahini

My brother's girlfriend follows a plant-based diet and so I initially made this aubergine dish for her at a family BBQ, alongside some chicken for everyone else, however, it was such a hit that we ended up whacking more aubergines on the grill and making enough for all of us. I prefer room temperature or even cool food in summer and tend to cook each dish at least a few hours before I intend on eating it. You can prepare the aubergines and sauce a day or so ahead of time and both will sit very happily in the fridge.

Serves 4
Time 30 minutes

3 medium aubergines
100ml olive oil
1 tsp smoked paprika
Generous pinch of salt

To serve
Green tahini **p. 188**
50g pistachios, roughly chopped
1 tbsp pink peppercorns
Small handful of mint leaves, roughly chopped

Roughly slice the aubergines into 1-cm rounds. In a small bowl, mix together the olive oil, smoked paprika and salt. Using a brush, coat both sides of the aubergine slices with the paprika oil.

Heat a griddle pan over a high heat. Once hot, cook the aubergines for 5–6 minutes, turning them halfway through, until they are well charred and soft. You'll need to work in batches. You could also do this on a BBQ.

To cook the aubergines in the oven, preheat the oven to 200°C fan and line two baking trays with parchment paper. Arrange the aubergine slices over the two trays ensuring there is a little space between each piece. Cook for 30 minutes or until golden and tender.

While the aubergines are cooking, prepare the green tahini following the instructions on page 188.

When ready to serve, spoon the green tahini onto a large plate and layer the aubergine slices on top. Scatter over the chopped pistachios, pink peppercorns and mint to finish.

Do aheads

Both the aubergines and green tahini can be prepared a day or even 2 days ahead and kept separately in the fridge. Be sure to pull them out at least 2 hours before serving so that the flavours have time to relax.

Goes well with
- Nectarines with burrata and pink peppercorns **p. 20**
- Pan-fried courgettes with mozzarella and pistachio butter **p. 54**
- Grilled cabbage with honey lime butter **p. 140**

Charred lettuce, two ways

I love charred lettuce, but I don't think we see it prepared this way often enough. It is such a quick and simple way to elevate an ingredient that can otherwise be a bit bland. Here, I have suggested two different ways of serving it. I love charred lettuce with whipped feta and a tomato-chilli salsa during high summer when the tomatoes are at their best, and with *ajo blanco* when it's a bit cooler, but both are delicious all year round.

On whipped feta with pickled chilli salsa

Serves 4–6
Time 25 minutes

4 baby gem lettuces
Olive oil
Coarse sea salt flakes
Whipped feta (**p. 192**)

For the tomato salsa

1 beef tomato, finely chopped

1 banana shallot, finely diced

2–3 pickled chillies, deseeded and finely chopped

Handful of parsley leaves, finely chopped

Juice of ½–1 lemon

Salt, to taste

Olive oil

Heat a griddle pan over a high heat or prepare the BBQ. Trim the base from the lettuces, then slice each one in half vertically. Rub each half with a little olive oil and sprinkle with sea salt flakes. Place the lettuces on the griddle pan or BBQ, cut side down, and cook for about 5 minutes until they have a good char. Turn each lettuce half over and cook for a further 4–5 minutes on the other side.

Make the whipped feta as per the recipe on page 192.

Combine all the ingredients for the salsa in a bowl with enough olive oil to achieve a spoonable consistency.

When ready to serve, spoon the whipped feta onto a platter, top with the charred lettuce and spoon over the salsa.

Do aheads

The whipped feta can be made a day ahead and stored in the fridge until serving.

Goes well with

- Butterflied leg of lamb with red wine vinegar **p. 146**
- Stuffed squid with tomatoes and feta **p. 144**
- Harissa honey chicken wings **p. 151**

With ajo blanco and spring onions

The dressing for this is taken from *ajo blanco*, a wonderful Spanish soup made with almonds, that is usually eaten chilled, as you would a gazpacho. Here, it is thicker with less water added. I have also increased the almonds and removed the breadcrumbs to make it gluten-free. It should be punchy and garlicky with a creamy consistency and is brilliant with the charred lettuce. Any leftovers are very good with grilled chicken, too. I've given the quantities of water and oil in grams, as I find it easier to simply weigh these directly into my blender.

Serves 4–6
Time 35 minutes

Handful of roasted Marcona almonds, roughly chopped, to serve
4 baby gem lettuces
2 bunches of spring onions
Olive oil
Coarse sea salt flakes

For the ajo blanco dressing

100g roasted Marcona almonds, roughly chopped
1 garlic clove, peeled
3–4 tbsp sherry vinegar
100g olive oil
120g water
Pinch of salt

If your almonds are not roasted, do this first. Either cook them in an oven set to 180°C fan for 10 minutes, or dry-fry them in a pan over a medium heat until golden. Allow them to cool, then roughly chop.

To make the dressing, place all the ingredients into a food processor, adding just 3 tablespoons of the vinegar to start with. Blitz until you have a creamy, thick dressing. Taste to season, adding more vinegar or sea salt flakes, if necessary. Set aside.

Heat a griddle pan over a medium-high heat or prepare the BBQ. Trim the base from the lettuces, then slice each one in half vertically. Rub each lettuce half and the spring onions with a little olive oil and sprinkle with salt. Place the lettuces on the griddle pan or BBQ, cut side down, along with the spring onions, and cook for about 5–6 minutes until they have a good char. Turn each lettuce half and the spring onions over and cook for a further 4–5 minutes on the other side.

Roughly chop the grilled spring onions.

Spoon the ajo blanco dressing over a large serving plate and arrange the charred lettuces on top. Scatter over the chopped spring onions and finish with a drizzle of olive oil, some sea salt flakes and the chopped almonds.

Do aheads

The ajo blanco dressing can be made a day ahead and stored in the fridge. Just remember to remove 30 minutes before serving and allow it to come to room temperature.

Goes well with

- Pan-fried chicken with chilli, tomatoes and mint **p. 58**
- Chicken with saffron and chickpeas **p. 104**
- Baked salmon with blood orange and chilli **p. 122**

Grilled cabbage with honey lime butter

Cabbage comes alive when exposed to a bit of fire, all it really needs is a bit of olive oil and salt and it is completely delicious. There is a trend to serve charred cabbage in halves or quarters, but I prefer to roughly chop it meaning everyone gets some of the good charred bits. If you can, this is best made on the BBQ, however, living in the UK, I have learnt that it is best to have a back-up plan should the weather decide to turn and so you will find instructions for how to cook it in the oven, too.

Serves 4–6
Time 45 minutes

2 hispi (pointed) cabbages
3 red chillies
Olive oil
Sea salt
50g butter
1 garlic clove, finely grated
1 tbsp runny honey
Grated zest and juice of 1 lime (plus extra grated zest to serve)
1 tbsp toasted sesame seeds (plus extra to serve)

Heat the oven grill or BBQ to a medium-high heat (between 200–250°C). If cooking in the oven, set the grill setting to 250°C.

Halve or quarter the cabbages, if very large. Keep the chillies whole. Rub everything in olive oil and season with sea salt.

If cooking on the BBQ, grill the chillies for 10 minutes or until well charred, then set aside to cool slightly. Grill the cabbages for 5 minutes on each side until charred, then move them over to the cooler outer edges of the BBQ for a further 10 minutes or until the centre is soft. If the BBQ is still very hot, wrap the cabbages in foil and leave them on the edges for 10 minutes.

If cooking in the oven, place the cabbage on a baking tray, cut side up, along with the chillies. Cook for 10 minutes, then turn the cabbages over and cook for a further 10 minutes or until both sides have a good char and the chillies are blackened in places.

Slice the chillies lengthways, remove the seeds and then roughly chop. Add the chopped chillies to a large saucepan with the butter and grated garlic. Melt the butter over a low-medium heat (heating the saucepan either on the BBQ or on the hob) until it begins to bubble and froth slightly, then stir through the honey, the lime zest and half its juice and a good pinch of sea salt. Remove from the heat.

Allow the cabbages to rest off the heat until cool enough to handle and then roughly chop. Add the chopped cabbage to the pan or a bowl and toss with the honey lime butter and toasted sesame seeds. Taste to check the seasoning, adding the remaining lime juice, if necessary.

Transfer everything to a large serving plate. Finish with more lime zest, sesame seeds and sea salt.

Goes well with
- Harissa sesame carrots with labneh **p. 95**
- Harissa honey chicken wings **p. 151**
- Butterflied leg of lamb with red wine vinegar **p. 146**

Charred spring onions with burrata, peas and dill

I love charred spring onions and often serve them as a side with just a squeeze of lemon and a lick of olive oil. They are also very good on toast with some creamy ricotta. Here, they are teamed with blanched peas, chopped dill and creamy burrata to create a dish with a little more substance. It is the sort of thing I love to eat for an easy Friday night supper, alongside some bubbly focaccia or sourdough, but it is also one that fares very well as a sharing dish or starter when entertaining. If you are doing a BBQ, just throw the spring onions on when the grill is empty for 10 minutes, otherwise, all they require is a flash on a griddle pan set over the hob.

Serves 4–6
Time 25 minutes

200g spring onions
200g frozen peas
Small bunch of dill (about 25g), finely chopped (plus extra to finish)
1 garlic clove, finely grated
Grated zest and juice of 1 unwaxed lemon
150g blob of burrata
Olive oil
Sea salt

If cooking on a BBQ, heat the BBQ to a medium-high heat (between 200–250°C). Alternatively, heat a griddle pan or dry frying pan over a medium-high heat on the hob.

Rinse the spring onions, wipe away any dust and remove any gnarly outer layers. There is no need to trim them. Pat the spring onions dry with kitchen paper, then rub them in olive oil and sprinkle with sea salt. Cook on the BBQ for about 5–6 minutes, turning every so often to ensure an even char. Allow to cool slightly. If cooking on the hob, cook for 5–6 minutes until evenly charred all over.

Meanwhile, blanch the peas in boiling water for 3 minutes, refresh in ice-cold water and then drain.

Roughly chop the charred spring onions into 1-cm pieces. Toss in a bowl with the blanched peas, chopped dill, grated garlic, lemon zest and the juice from half the lemon. Season with a good pinch of sea salt and a generous glug of olive oil. Taste to check the seasoning, adjusting with more lemon juice, olive oil and sea salt, if needed.

Arrange the vegetables over a serving platter and then tear over the burrata. Finish with an extra drizzle of olive oil, some more sea salt and a little extra chopped dill, if you like.

Do aheads

You can prepare the peas and spring onions ahead of time, if you like, and keep everything chilled separately until 30 minutes before tossing it all together and serving.

Goes well with

- Crispy chicken thighs with lemon and pink peppercorns **p. 119**
- Pan-fried chicken with chilli, tomatoes and mint **p. 58**
- Wholegrain focaccia **p. 202**

Stuffed squid with tomatoes and feta

One of my favourite restaurants is a taverna called Sotos on the Greek island of Leros. Blue-painted tables and chairs stretch out onto the steely-grey pebbled beach, while a small kitchen with a huge stone oven and open grill sits on the other side of the road. It serves some of the best seafood I have ever eaten, and a dish that has stayed with me was a plate of squid stuffed with red peppers, ouzo and feta. Squid for me definitely falls into the category of something people are nervous of cooking, but should try because it is so much simpler than it seems. I use tomatoes here, which give a softer, saucier filling. I have also added fennel seeds, firstly, because I love them, but also because they have a slight aniseed note that echoes the flavour of ouzo. This is best cooked on an open grill, such as a BBQ, but I have included instructions for a griddle pan (my preference) or the oven, too.

Serves 4–6
Time 45 minutes

1 tsp fennel seeds
Olive oil
400g cherry tomatoes
1 garlic clove, crushed
1 tsp dried oregano
150g feta
750g squid, cleaned
Sea salt
Freshly cracked black pepper

To serve
Lemon wedges, for squeezing over

Do aheads
- The tomato and feta filling can be made a day ahead and refrigerated.
- Once the squid is stuffed, they can sit in the fridge for up to 6 hours.

Goes well with
- Tomato salad p. 41
- Grilled aubergines with green tahini p. 134
- Charred lettuce, two ways p. 137

In a dry frying pan set over a low-medium heat, toast the fennel seeds for about 3 minutes or until they just begin to smell fragrant. Transfer to a plate.

Increase the heat to medum-high and add 1 tablespoon of olive oil to the pan. Add the cherry tomatoes, then shake the pan a few times to coat them in the oil. Leave the tomatoes to cook for 2 minutes without stirring or moving the pan – they should char and blacken on the bottom. Now give the pan a shake and cook the tomatoes for a further 5 minutes, shaking every so often until the skins start to split.

Using the back of a spatula, break down the tomatoes so they release their juices. Add the toasted fennel seeds, crushed garlic and dried oregano to the pan and cook gently for 5–6 minutes or until the tomatoes have reduced slightly. Transfer the cooked tomatoes to a mixing bowl and allow to cool to room temperature.

Once the tomatoes have cooled, stir through 2 tablespoons of olive oil, a good pinch of sea salt and some freshly cracked black pepper.

Place the feta in a small bowl and, using the back of a fork, crush it until roughly broken down; don't worry if a few larger pieces remain, but remember you will need to be able to spoon it into the squid. Stir the feta through the tomatoes.

Using a teaspoon, fill the squid with the tomato-feta mixture. This is a bit fiddly and so I sometimes use my hands rather than a spoon. Do not worry if some of the mixture ends up on the outside of the squid rather than inside. Seal the squid with cocktail sticks, threading the wooden sticks over and under through the open base of the body. Place in the fridge to chill until you are ready to cook.

Heat the BBQ to about 230°C, heat a griddle pan over a high heat, or set your oven to the grill setting on the highest heat.

Drizzle the stuffed squid and tentacles with a generous amount of olive oil. Cook on the BBQ or the griddle pan for about 3–4 minutes on either side. Alternatively, cook in the oven under the grill for about 10 minutes.

Transfer the squid to a serving plate, drizzle over more olive oil and serve with fresh lemon wedges for squeezing over.

Butterflied leg of lamb with red wine vinegar

I don't eat a lot of red meat at home so when I do I like to make the most of it and buy the best quality I can. This is such a crowd-pleaser and I find a little goes a long way. There is usually a natural unevenness to a butterflied leg of lamb, too, which means that everyone gets meat cooked to their liking. The key to this lamb dish is the vinegar, which helps to tenderise the meat more than anything else. I find lamb quite a 'meaty' meat that stands up well to bold seasoning. I tend to marinate the leg of lamb the night before so that it gets a good 14 hours, but I don't advise marinating it longer than 24 hours as I find you lose the texture of the meat.

Serves 6

Time 40 minutes, plus 12–14 hours marinating and 10 minutes resting

1.5kg boneless leg of lamb, butterflied (ask your butcher to do this)

Olive oil (if cooking lamb in oven)

For the marinade

2 tsp fennel seeds

2 tsp cumin seeds

2 tsp ground cinnamon

2 tbsp oregano leaves, finely chopped

2 tbsp thyme leaves

4 garlic cloves, crushed

Good pinch of salt

6 tbsp sherry vinegar

8 tbsp olive oil

Grated zest and juice of ½ unwaxed lemon

Do aheads

I find a long marinate really benefits this and try to ensure it gets 12 hours.

Goes well with

- Loaded feta with peach, olives and herbs **p. 28**
- Carrot and coriander salad **p. 24**
- Charred lettuce, two ways: on whipped feta | with ajo blanco **p. 137**

In a dry frying pan set over a gentle heat, toast the fennel seeds and cumin seeds for 3 minutes or until they just begin to smell fragrant. Allow them to cool slightly, then crush in a pestle and mortar.

Add the toasted crushed spices to a freezer bag large enough to hold the lamb, along with the remaining ingredients for the marinade. Give everything a shake or a squish to combine the marinade. Add the lamb and manipulate the marinade so that all the meat is well coated. Transfer to the fridge to marinate for at least 6 hours or ideally overnight.

Remove the lamb from the fridge an hour before cooking to allow it to come to room temperature. This is crucial, otherwise you will end up with tough, chewy meat.

If cooking on the BBQ, heat the BBQ to high. Cook the lamb on the BBQ, fat side down, for about 14 minutes. Turn over and cook the other side for about 8 minutes or until the meat is done to your liking. You will find some parts more done than others due to the uneven nature of the cut of meat – I find this works out well as there are usually some who prefer their meat medium while others prefer it well-done. Remove the lamb from the heat and allow it to rest under a loose sheet of foil for 10 minutes before slicing.

If cooking in the oven, before marinating, cut the lamb into 2 or 3 pieces so that it fits into a pan. Preheat the oven to 190°C fan. Place an oven rack over a roasting tray.

Heat a generous glug of olive oil in a large frying pan and sear a piece of the lamb for about 3 minutes on either side until it is golden brown. Repeat with the remaining lamb piece(s).

Place the seared lamb pieces on the rack over the tray fat-side-up and cook in the oven for 20–25 minutes for medium-rare or 30–35 minutes for well-done. Remove the lamb from the oven, loosely cover with a sheet of foil and allow the meat to rest for 10 minutes.

When ready to serve, slice the lamb and arrange on a serving platter.

Grilled bream with charred spring onion salsa

My death row dish would be some iteration of grilled fish with lemon. Every year, when we finally get round to dusting off the BBQ, I am reminded of just how good such a simple dish can be. All you really need alongside BBQ'd fish is a fat wedge of lemon, but I love the addition of this salsa. The charred spring onions are both smoky and sweet, which is the perfect match for grilled bream (although you can use sea bass, if you prefer). Make sure you pat the fish dry before giving it a good rub in olive oil – this will help you to achieve a crispy skin. *Pictured overleaf.*

Serves 4

Time 35–50 minutes

4 bream or sea bass, scaled, gutted and cleaned

Olive oil

Sea salt

4 unwaxed lemons, 3 sliced and 1 halved

Handful of fresh bay leaves or bunch of rosemary sprigs

4 garlic cloves, peeled and thinly sliced

For the salsa

200g spring onions

Olive oil

Sea salt

Small bunch of parsley or coriander (about 25g), leaves finely chopped

1 garlic clove, finely grated

2 green chillies, deseeded and finely chopped

Juice of ½–1 lemon

Do aheads

The salsa can be made a couple of hours ahead.

Goes well with

- Tomato Salad (also pictured overleaf) **p. 41**
- New potatoes with anchovy chive butter **p. 77**
- Salsa verde salad **p. 25**

Heat the BBQ to a medium-high heat or preheat the oven to 200°C fan.

First, make the salsa. Rinse the spring onions, wipe away any dust and remove any gnarly outer layers. There is no need to trim them. Pat the spring onions dry with kitchen paper, then rub them in olive oil and sprinkle with sea salt. Cook the spring onions on the BBQ or in the hot oven on a baking tray for 5–6 minutes or until nicely charred – they should be blackened in places with a soft centre.

Allow the spring onions to cool slightly, before roughly chopping them and combining with the remaining salsa ingredients. Add enough olive oil to reach a spoonable consistency and adjust the amounts of lemon juice and salt to taste. Set aside.

When ready to cook the fish, check the temperature of the BBQ and allow it to come to a medium-high heat (between 200–250°C). If cooking in the oven, check the temperature is 200°C fan and oil a large baking tray.

Ensure the fish are clean, with any remnants of their guts removed, then pat dry with kitchen paper. Using a sharp knife, make 3 or 4 slits on each side of the fish. Rub the fish in a generous amount of olive oil and season well with sea salt. Add a couple of lemon slices and 2–3 fresh bay leaves or rosemary sprigs, and a few garlic slices into each cavity.

If grilling on the BBQ, cook the fish, without moving, over the hottest part of the BBQ for 5–6 minutes on one side, then flip over and cook for a further 5–6 minutes. The flesh should be flaky and easily pull away from the bone. Add the halved lemon to the BBQ, cut side down, and allow it to cook for about 5 minutes or until the cut side is charred.

If cooking in the oven, lay a couple more slices of lemon onto the tray under where you intend to place the fish (this will stop it sticking). Place the prepared fish on top of the lemon slices and bake in the oven for 20–25 minutes or until the fish has cooked through. I switch the oven to the grill setting for the last 5 minutes of the cooking time to get the skin extra crispy.

Transfer the fish to a platter and spoon over the spring onion salsa.

Harissa honey chicken wings

A good chicken wing should be saucy and the meat should be tender and juicy. I think these are perfect and they are incredibly simple to make. You start by cooking the wings in the oven in just a simple toss of oil, salt and pepper to get some colour and char, then they get another stint in the oven after being tossed in a sticky spicy glaze. The core of the glaze is harissa paste, which is readily available these days at most supermarkets. In terms of spices, there is smoked paprika for smokiness, cayenne pepper for optional heat (the harissa already has a good kick) and cinnamon for subtle warmth. The cinnamon is non-negotiable and really pulls the flavours together. The stickiness comes from honey; there is no need to use the really good stuff for this, a squeezy bottle is fine.

Serves 4
Time 40 minutes

12 chicken wings (ask your butcher to cut them into drums and flats as it saves you doing it at home)
4 tbsp olive oil
Sea salt and freshly ground black pepper

For the glaze
80g runny honey
80g rose harissa paste (I use Belazu)
2 garlic cloves, crushed
1 tbsp olive oil
1 tbsp apple cider vinegar
3 tsp smoked paprika
1 tsp cayenne pepper (optional, leave out if you prefer less heat)
1 tsp ground cinnamon
1 tsp coarse sea salt flakes

To serve
1 tbsp toasted sesame seeds (optional)

Preheat the oven to 220°C fan. Line a baking tray with foil and sit a grill rack over the tray. The marinade is sticky so this is to protect your pan more than anything, but it also ensures that the wings colour all over with no need to turn them.

If the chicken wings are whole, cut them into drums and flats. Using a sharp knife, slice through the joint so that you have a mini drumstick and a flat wing.

Place the chicken pieces in a bowl and toss them in the olive oil with plenty of salt and black pepper. Arrange the wings evenly on the rack set over the tray. Cook the chicken in the oven for 15 minutes while you make the glaze.

Combine all the ingredients for the glaze together in a large bowl.

After they have cooked for 15 minutes, tong the chicken pieces into the bowl with the glaze and give them a good toss, ensuring they are all coated. Return the chicken to the rack, spacing them apart. I toss the chicken pieces in the glaze in batches as they are easier to handle. Drizzle any excess glaze onto the wings, prioritising those that look a little bare. Return the chicken to the oven for a further 10 minutes. The wings should be glossy and charred in places.

Sprinkle the chicken wings with the toasted sesame seeds and eat them while they are hot.

Do aheads
The harissa glaze can be made a day ahead.

Goes well with
- Za'atar cabbage, fennel, apple slaw **p. 40**
- Queen Caesar salad **p. 23**
- Fruit and nut rice **p. 87**

SUGARED

STRAWBERRY FLAPJACK TART
157

FLOURLESS CHOCOLATE MERINGUE CAKE
158

PISTACHIO TIRAMISU
161

ROASTED CHERRY ALMOND TART
164

NO-CHURN MISO CARAMEL PECAN ICE CREAM
166

NO-CHURN RASPBERRY RIPPLE ICE CREAM
167

APRICOT, RICOTTA AND ALMOND CAKE
170

BAKED FIGS AND PLUMS WITH WHIPPED HONEY YOGURT AND AMARETTI
172

PEAR AND HAZELNUT FRANGIPANE GALETTE
175

CHOCOLATE MARMALADE TART
176

CAMPARI AND BLOOD ORANGE JELLY
178

MOLTEN CHOCOLATE SKILLET BROWNIE
179

SPICED GINGER CAKE WITH WHIPPED MASCARPONE
181

I have always loved making puddings. When I was 15, I set up my own cake company (complete with hand-written business cards on which I drew my 'cake of the month'). It was a successful business until the summer holidays ran out and I could no longer spend my days cracking eggs and whisking buttercream amidst a plume of icing sugar. I felt so bad for letting people down that I gave away the recipes to my best customers (on hand-illustrated A4 sheets of card), and when the summer came round again, most of my then customers were sending me blurry photos of their own creations. It was the first of many bad business moves, but even then I didn't really mind. I was just glad that people were making pudding. It's fair to say that baking is not like cooking. In many ways it does not allow for personal interpretation, and usually if it goes wrong, there are limited ways to bring it back. But as with most things, one of the key ingredients to making good puddings is confidence. I have included some of my favourite puddings in this chapter. Most require very little technical skill and, should things go awry, can usually be dressed up in some way so that they're still the belle of the ball. Perhaps it's because this is the way that I like to cook, without stress and without panic, but I think it is also confidence. Confidence that if the pastry has cracked and the berries have seeped out a little, the tart is still delicious. Confidence that any pudding, even the laziest of puddings, is far better than no pudding.

Strawberry flapjack tart

It is always a joyful moment when strawberries come into season. Pairing them with ricotta may seem an odd choice, but believe me when I say it works. Creamy and cool, it is the perfect filling between a topping of juicy, sweet strawberries and the chewy flapjack base. I like to keep it simple and fresh by just adding lemon zest to the ricotta, but you could add a teaspoon of vanilla paste or honey if you like it a little sweeter. Feel free to make this a day ahead. This tart is best enjoyed after an hour or so in the fridge and will keep well for up to 3 days.

Serves 10
Time 35 minutes, plus cooling

For the base
100g rolled porridge oats
150g plain flour, or white spelt flour
1 tsp bicarbonate of soda
Pinch of coarse sea salt flakes
100g unsalted butter
100g light soft brown sugar
1 tbsp runny honey

For the filling
2 x 250g tubs of ricotta
Grated zest of 2 unwaxed lemons
400g strawberries

You will also need an 8inch, 20-cm springform cake tin.

Preheat the oven to 180°C fan and line a 20-cm springform cake tin with parchment paper. I use a large sheet of parchment for this so that it covers the base and sides.

In a medium bowl, whisk together the oats, flour, bicarbonate of soda and sea salt flakes.

In a saucepan set over a low heat, melt together the butter, sugar and honey until all the sugar has dissolved.

Pour the melted butter into the bowl and stir it through the oat mixture until well combined.

Scrape the oat mixture into the lined tin. Using the back of a metal spoon dipped in water, spread and press the oat mixture to cover the base and create a 2-cm border up the sides of the tin.

Bake the tart base in the oven for 12 minutes or until golden brown. The base will puff up during cooking – do not be alarmed by this – and the sides may shrink slightly. While the tart is still warm, use a spoon to push it back into place, pressing the sides up the tin and encouraging them to form a raised border. Allow the base to cool completely, then remove it from the tin.

Meanwhile, whisk together the ricotta and lemon zest. Wash and hull the strawberries, removing their green tops. Depending on their size, either halve the strawberries or leave them whole.

Once the tart base has cooled, spread over the lemony ricotta and top with the strawberries. Keep chilled until ready to serve.

Do aheads
The tart base can be made a day ahead, but I recommend adding the lemony ricotta and strawberries just before serving.

Flourless chocolate meringue cake

This is a rich pudding that is a guaranteed showstopper. The fudgy chocolate cake layer is part-baked before being topped with the meringue mixture, which is then returned to the oven until the meringue has a crisp, shiny top. It is wonderfully decadent and, in my family, it is often made for celebrations in place of a conventional birthday cake. It is delicious on its own, but I love it with a little crème fraîche to offset the richness.

Serves 12
Time 1 hour 25 minutes

For the chocolate cake
300g dark chocolate (70% cocoa), chopped or broken
150g unsalted butter, cut into cubes
5 large eggs, separated, plus 2 large egg yolks
175g caster sugar
Pinch of coarse sea salt flakes

For the meringue topping
2 large egg whites
120g caster sugar
1 tbsp unsweetened cocoa powder
1 tbsp cornflour
1 tsp apple cider vinegar

To serve
Crème fraîche (optional)

You will also need a 20-cm springform cake tin.

Preheat the oven to 170°C fan and line the base and sides of a 20-cm springform cake tin with parchment paper.

First, make the chocolate cake. In a heatproof bowl set over a saucepan of simmering water, melt the chocolate and butter together, stirring to combine. Remove the bowl from the heat and allow the chocolate mixture to cool slightly.

Meanwhile, whisk the 5 egg whites. In a large, grease-free bowl using an electric whisk, beat the egg whites with the sugar until they reach a marshmallow consistency with slightly droopy peaks. Set aside.

Once cool, beat all 7 egg yolks into the chocolate mixture along with the sea salt flakes. Now fold in one-third of the beaten egg whites to loosen the chocolate mixture. Next, transfer the chocolate mixture into the larger bowl with the remaining egg whites and gently fold together until everything is well incorporated and a mousse-like texture.

Scrape the cake batter evenly into the prepared tin. Bake the cake in the centre of the oven for 20 minutes or until slightly risen and a crust has formed on top. (Don't worry if the middle of the cake wobbles a little.) After 20 minutes, remove the cake from the oven and increase the oven temperature to 180°C fan.

While the cake is cooling slightly, make the meringue topping. In a large, grease-free bowl using an electric whisk, beat the remaining 2 egg whites until thick and frothy. Slowly add the sugar, a tablespoon at a time, continuing to whisk until you have a strong meringue that holds stiff peaks. Sift in the cocoa powder and cornflour, then gently fold in with the apple cider vinegar using a metal spoon.

Spoon the meringue mixture over the cake and return to the oven for a further 35 minutes or until the meringue puffs up and has a shiny top. (Don't worry if the meringue cracks or slightly mushrooms over the top.)

Transfer the cake still in the tin to a wire rack and allow to cool for 5 minutes. Using your hands, push up any meringue that has collapsed over the edge of the tin to encourage it to collapse inwards – there is no need to be too precious with this, it is meant to look a little dramatic. Run a knife around the inside edge of the tin to loosen the sides of the cake and release the sides of the springform cake tin. Allow the cake to cool before removing from the tin and serving.

Serve slices of the cake with crème fraîche, if you like.

Pistachio tiramisu

Growing up, tiramisu was my favourite pudding. In fact, it still is. However, by some cruel twist of fate, I have married a man who does not like tiramisu. While that is fine in a restaurant (more for me), it does mean that I usually only make it at home when we have people coming over. I made this version in an attempt to sway my husband as he loves pistachio anything. It sort of worked. His response was 'I don't hate it'. Just the sort of thing you want to hear when you've lovingly made pudding. But don't take his word for it, take mine instead – it is delicious.

Serves 12

Time 25 minutes, plus at least 4 hours chilling

2 eggs, separated, plus 1 egg white

100g caster sugar

450g mascarpone

175g pistachio paste or pistachio cream

150ml strong brewed coffee, cooled

75ml coffee liqueur (I use Kahlúa)

75ml almond liqueur, such as Amaretto (or you can use Frangelico for a hazelnut flavour or Cointreau for an orange flavour)

About 30 savoiardi (ladyfinger) biscuits

75g pistachios, roughly chopped

You will also need a deep bowl or serving dish. I use a round glass trifle bowl which is 28-cm wide and 7-cm deep.

In a large bowl using an electric whisk, beat the 2 egg yolks with 50g of the caster sugar until pale and fluffy.

Then, switching to a handheld whisk so as not to overbeat them, beat in the mascarpone and pistachio paste/cream until smooth.

In a separate large, grease-free bowl, whisk the 3 egg whites until frothy. Add the remaining 50g of caster sugar and beat to firm peaks.

Fold half the beaten egg whites into the pistachio-mascarpone mixture to loosen it, then gently fold in the rest until you have a light, fluffy mix.

Combine the coffee, coffee liqueur and almond liqueur in a small bowl or measuring jug. One by one, briefly dunk each savoiardi biscuit in the liquid, turning once to ensure it is moistened evenly.

Arrange a layer of the coffee-dipped savoiardi biscuits over the base of your serving dish. Spoon in half of the pistachio-mascarpone mixture and gently spread to cover the biscuits. Arrange another layer of the remaining coffee-dipped savoiardi biscuits over the top, then gently spread over the remaining pistachio-mascarpone mixture. To finish, scatter over the chopped pistachios.

Allow the tiramisu to rest in the fridge for at least 4 hours or ideally overnight, before serving.

Roasted cherry almond tart

There are few puddings more delicious than an almond tart. The best almond tart (in my opinion) is to be found at Quo Vadis in Soho, London. Chef proprietor Jeremy Lee showed me that what makes a really good almond tart is the chilling – chill the pastry, chill the frangipane – and don't be tempted to rush. Jeremy also taught me not to level out the frangipane when filling the tart shell. Leave the edges rough as you scoop it in; it will settle as it cooks, creating the perfect crisp shell. I make this in various iterations throughout the year. Around Christmastime, I love to add a layer of mincemeat or roasted cranberries, while during the summer, when cherries are in season, I make it this way. Roasting the cherries intensifies their flavour but also helps them to release some of their juice before they bake in the tart, so there is no soggy bottom.

Serves 8–12

Time 2 hours, plus at least 2 hours 30 minutes chilling

1 quantity of sweet shortcrust pastry (**p. 209**)

For the frangipane and filling

200g blanched almonds

200g unsalted butter, at room temperature

200g caster sugar

2 large eggs, lightly beaten

2 tbsp plain flour

For the roasted cherries

300g fresh cherries

Juice of ½ unwaxed lemon

1 tbsp caster sugar

2 tbsp plain flour

To serve

Icing sugar, to dust

Crème fraîche or loosely whipped double cream (optional)

You will also need a 23-cm loose-based, fluted tart tin.

First, make the pastry, following the instructions on page 209.

Next, make the frangipane. In a food processor, pulse the blanched almonds until they resemble coarse, uneven breadcrumbs. The aim is to retain some texture here. Set aside.

In a large bowl using an electric whisk, cream together the butter and sugar, then beat in the eggs. Gently fold in the chopped almonds and the flour. Place the frangipane in the fridge to chill for at least 1 hour.

Meanwhile, preheat the oven to 170°C fan.

Remove the stones from the cherries either using a cherry pitter or a sharp knife to halve them. Toss the pitted cherries with the lemon juice and sugar on a baking tray. Roast the cherries for 20 minutes or until they have released their juices and are sticky and glossy. Switch off the oven and allow the cherries to cool to room temperature, then transfer them to the fridge to chill for at least 1 hour.

Lightly dust a clean work surface with a little flour and roll out the pastry to a thickness of 3-mm. Line a 23-cm loose-based, fluted tart tin with the pastry. Trim any excess pastry overhanging the edges of the tin and place it in the fridge to chill for 1 hour.

Once everything is sufficiently chilled, preheat the oven to 170°C fan and place a large, flat baking tray in the middle of the oven to warm.

In a clean bowl, toss the roasted cherries with the of flour, leaving behind any juices the cherries have released (keep these for drizzling onto ice cream or stirring into a gin or vodka tonic). Dot the cherries over the base of the chilled pastry case. Spoon the chilled frangipane over the cherries. Resist the urge to flatten the frangipane down – allow it to be uneven. (The rough edges are how you achieve a lovely crisp top.)

Do aheads

The chilling time is key to a good almond tart. I tend to make both the pastry, frangipane and roasted cherries the night before, so they are sufficiently chilled before assembling and baking the tart.

Place the tart tin on the preheated baking tray in the oven and bake for 1 hour 10 minutes. (The tray will catch any butter that escapes from the tart.) When the tart is cooked, both the pastry and almond filling should be golden brown. If the frangipane is browning too much, cover loosely with foil.

Transfer the tart in its tin to a wire rack and allow to cool completely before removing from the tin, dusting with icing sugar. Serve with crème fraîche or loosely whipped double cream, if you like.

No-churn miso caramel pecan ice cream

I have used this no-churn method of making ice cream for years. Technically, this is more of a semifreddo, but scooped up and decorated with some roasted pecans or served with fresh strawberries, who is to know? There is zero elbow grease required for this recipe. The order in which everything is added to the bowl is crucial, however, once it is whipped up, it goes into the freezer and that's it. *Pictured overleaf.*

Serves 10–12

Time 45 minutes, plus chilling and at least 6 hours or overnight freezing

90g toasted pecans, roughly chopped

4 eggs, separated

100g caster sugar

300ml double cream

3 tbsp orange liqueur, such as Cointreau (or you can use Frangelico for a hazelnut flavour or Amaretto for an almond flavour)

For the miso caramel

200g caster sugar

100ml double cream

1 tbsp unsalted butter

1 heaped tbsp white miso paste

You will also need a freezer-safe container, such as a 450-g loaf tin or Pyrex dish, measuring about 20-cm by 14-cm.

Do aheads

The miso caramel can be made the day before and kept in the fridge. The pecans can also be toasted the day before.

First, make the miso caramel. Place the sugar in a heavy-based frying pan with 3 tablespoons of cold water and stir to combine. Over a medium heat, without touching the pan or stirring, heat the sugar until all the grains have dissolved and it begins to bubble. Cook for about 4–5 minutes or until the caramel is golden and bubbling. Once it begins to turn golden, you can gently swirl the pan, but do not stir at this point.

Once the caramel is golden brown, switch off the heat and stir in the cream. Using a whisk, incorporate the butter and miso paste until thick and glossy. Transfer the miso caramel to a small jug or bowl and place in the fridge to chill for 30 minutes.

If your pecans are not toasted, do this now. Preheat the oven to 170°C fan. Spread the pecans over a baking tray and toast in the oven for 10 minutes or until golden. Allow to cool before roughly chopping.

In a large, grease-free bowl using an electric whisk, beat the egg whites until thick and frothy. Slowly add the sugar, a tablespoon at a time, continuing to whisk until you have stiff peaks. Set aside.

Pour the cream into a separate large bowl. Using a handheld balloon whisk (not an electric one), whip the cream just until soft, droopy peaks form. Do not over-whip the cream or the ice cream will be lumpy.

In a small bowl, beat the egg yolks using a fork. In a separate small bowl, combine 2 heaped tablespoons of the miso caramel with the liqueur. Fold the miso caramel-liqueur mixture into the beaten egg yolks, then fold the egg yolks into the whipped cream in the large bowl.

Next, fold one-quarter of the egg whites into the whipped cream to loosen it. Add the remaining egg whites and gently fold in. Halfway through, add one-third of the remaining miso caramel and most of the chopped pecans, then fold until incorporated.

Pour half of the ice-cream mixture into a freezer-safe container. (I use a 450g loaf tin.) Drizzle over a heaped tablespoon of the remaining miso caramel and, using a cocktail stick or skewer, swirl it through. Pour in the remaining ice-cream mixture and swirl through the remaining miso caramel as before. Scatter over the remaining chopped pecans. Loosely cover the top with parchment paper. (This will avoid the decorated top lifting off when the cling film or lid is removed later.) Wrap the container in cling film or cover with a lid. Freeze for at least 6 hours or ideally overnight before serving.

No-churn raspberry ripple ice cream

Much like the No-Churn Miso Caramel Pecan Ice Cream on page 166, this recipe is foolproof. The key is the order in which things are whipped and folded together, but the method itself is simple and calls for no fancy equipment or multiple trips to the freezer to whisk up frozen cream. Most no-churn ice cream recipes call for condensed milk, but it is something I rarely have in the cupboard, so instead I make mine with eggs. The result is slightly lighter but wonderfully creamy with streaks of vibrant raspberry running through.

Serves 10–12

Time 45 minutes, plus chilling and at least 6 hours or overnight freezing

400g fresh or frozen raspberries (I use frozen)

100g caster sugar (plus an extra 3 tbsp)

4 eggs, separated

300ml double cream

1 vanilla pod (or 1 tsp vanilla extract)

3 tbsp almond liqueur, such as Amaretto (or you can use Cointreau for an orange flavour)

You will also need a freezer-safe container, such as a 450g loaf tin or Pyrex dish, measuring about 20-cm by 14-cm.

Put 300g of the raspberries into a saucepan with the 3 tablespoons of caster sugar. Place the pan over a medium heat until the raspberries have broken down – you may need to add a splash of cold water to get them going. Once they have broken down, pass the raspberries through a sieve to remove the seeds.

Clean the saucepan, then return the raspberry coulis to the pan and bring to a simmer for 5–10 minutes or until the coulis has thickened enough so that your finger leaves a mark when dragged through the mixture when coating the back of a spoon. Transfer the coulis to a small bowl or jug, then place in the fridge to chill.

In a large, grease-free bowl using an electric whisk, beat the egg whites until thick and frothy. Slowly add the remaining sugar, a tablespoon at a time, continuing to whisk until you have a strong meringue that holds stiff peaks. Set aside.

Pour the cream into a separate large bowl. Using a sharp knife, split open the vanilla pod lengthways and scrape the seeds into the cream. Using a handheld balloon whisk (not an electric one), whip the cream just until soft, droopy peaks form. Do not over-whip the cream or the ice cream will be lumpy.

In a small bowl, beat the egg yolks using a fork and then stir in the liqueur. Fold the egg yolks into the whipped cream in the large bowl.

Next, fold one-quarter of the egg white mixture into the whipped cream to loosen it. Add the remaining egg whites and gently fold to combine.

Keeping about 1 tablespoon back to decorate, gently fold through almost all of the chilled raspberry coulis along with most of the remaining raspberries to create a ripple effect.

Pour the ice-cream mixture into a freezer-safe container. (I use a Pyrex dish measuring about 20-cm by 14-cm.) Drizzle over the remaining raspberry coulis and, using a toothpick or skewer, create a marbled pattern over the surface. Sprinkle over the remaining raspberries and loosely cover the top with parchment paper. (This will avoid the decorated top lifting off when the cling film or lid is removed later.) Wrap the container in cling film or cover with a lid. Freeze for at least 6 hours or ideally overnight before serving.

Do aheads

The raspberry coulis can be made the day before.

Apricot, ricotta and almond cake

We enjoyed ten blissful days in Sardinia on our honeymoon. Every morning we would buy fat, juicy tomatoes, vast bouquets of basil and always a huge bucket of the freshest, creamiest ricotta. In the evening, we would sit in the garden and enjoy large scoops of the ricotta with fresh apricots and a spoonful of honey. It is a pudding that I have often tried to recreate, although never quite been able to match. In a way, this cake is an ode to that holiday. It is one that works well for an afternoon treat or as a summery pudding with the ricotta bringing a wonderful creaminess to the cake. I love to add a splash of Amaretto for an additional almondy kick, but it is delicious with just a splash of vanilla extract.

Serves 8–10
Time 1 hour 25 minutes

- 200g white spelt flour (or plain flour)
- 2 tsp baking powder
- Pinch of fine sea salt
- Grated zest of 1 unwaxed lemon
- 150g unsalted butter, softened
- 225g golden caster sugar
- 250g ricotta, strained
- 1 tsp vanilla extract
- 2 tbsp almond liqueur, such as Amaretto (optional)
- 3 large eggs, lightly beaten
- 6–8 ripe apricots, halved and stoned
- 50g flaked almonds
- Icing sugar, to dust

You will also need a 20-cm springform cake tin.

Preheat the oven to 170°C fan and line the base and sides of a 20-cm springform cake tin with parchment paper.

In a medium bowl, whisk together the flour, baking powder, salt and lemon zest. Set aside.

In a separate bowl, using an electric whisk or stand mixer, beat together the butter and caster sugar until light and fluffy. Beat in the ricotta, with the beaters set to the slowest setting, followed by the vanilla extract and almond liqueur (if using). Slowly pour in the beaten eggs, whisking continuously.

Using a silicone spatula or wooden spoon, fold the flour mixture into the ricotta mixture.

Scrape the cake batter into the lined tin and level the surface. Arrange the apricots, cut side down, over the surface of the batter and then scatter over the flaked almonds.

Bake the cake in the oven for 50–60 minutes or until the cake is springy to the touch and a skewer or cocktail stick inserted into the centre comes out with just a few crumbs on it. Allow the cake to cool in the tin for 5 minutes, then remove the sides of the tin and leave to cool completely. Remove the base of the tin, dust the top of the cake with icing sugar before serving in slices.

Baked figs and plums with whipped honey yogurt and amaretti

This is a perfect pudding to make when you don't have a huge amount of time or energy. Figs and plums really come alive when baked and a hint of vanilla brings a wonderful extra layer of flavour. Vanilla pods are not inexpensive, but they are worth it. I use one to flavour both the fruit and the whipped honey yogurt cream here. To make the most of the pod, post-baking, you can add it to a jar of caster sugar to make vanilla sugar. The whipped honey yogurt cream is a lighter take on a traditional vanilla whipped cream. I find the slight tanginess that the yogurt brings offsets the juicy sweetness of the figs and plums perfectly.

Serves 4–6
Time 45 minutes

4–6 ripe figs
4–6 ripe plums, halved and stoned
1 vanilla pod
150g full-fat Greek yogurt
Juice of 1 orange
2 tbsp runny honey
150ml double cream
About 4 amaretti biscuits, to serve (optional)

Preheat the oven to 180°C fan.

Using a sharp knife, score the figs in a cross from the stem end, allowing the knife to go just halfway down the fruit. Place the scored figs in a deep roasting dish with the plums.

Using a sharp knife, split open the vanilla pod lengthways and scrape half of the seeds into the dish with the fruit. Scrape the rest of the seeds into a medium bowl with the yogurt.

Squeeze the juice of the orange over the fruit, then drizzle with the honey and toss well to combine. Arrange the figs and plums so they are cut side up and then nestle the vanilla pod in between the fruit. Bake the fruit in the oven for 25 minutes or until soft. Allow to cool.

For the whipped honey yogurt cream, add the cream to the bowl with the vanilla and yogurt. Using a handheld balloon whisk (not an electric one), whip the cream just until soft, droopy peaks form.

When ready to serve, spoon the whipped honey yogurt cream onto a serving dish or dishes, top with the baked figs and plums along with any fruit juices from the roasting dish. Crush over the amaretti biscuits (if using) and serve immediately.

Pear and hazelnut frangipane galette

I adore the ease of a galette. There is no frill, no fuss. In fact, the wonkier the better. A galette is essentially a rustic open pie and is the pudding I lean on most when I'm short of time. I love to use stone fruits such as apricots and plums in the summer, but in the winter apples and pears are my go-to. This one has an added layer of buttery hazelnut frangipane, which makes it a little more indulgent.

Serves 8–10

Time 1 hour 20 minutes, plus at least 2 hours chilling

1 quantity of sweet shortcrust pastry (**p. 209**), keep hold of the reserved egg white for a pastry wash
3 firm, ripe pears
Juice of ¼ lemon
Egg white, beaten, to brush
Caster sugar, to sprinkle

For the frangipane
50g blanched almonds
50g blanched hazelnuts
100g butter, softened
100g caster sugar
1 large egg, lightly beaten
1 tsp vanilla extract

To serve
Icing sugar
Vanilla ice cream (optional)

First, make the pastry following the instructions on page 209.

Next, make the frangipane. In a food processor, pulse the blanched almonds until they resemble coarse breadcrumbs. Do the same with the hazelnuts. Set aside.

Cream together the butter and sugar, then beat in the egg and vanilla extract. Fold in the ground almonds and hazelnuts. Place the frangipane in the fridge to chill for at least 1 hour.

Once everything is sufficiently chilled, preheat the oven to 180°C fan and line a large baking tray with parchment paper.

Peel and quarter the pears, then trim away the core. Keeping the quarter together as best you can so that you can fan out the fruit when assembling, slice each quarter into thin slices. Squeeze over a little lemon juice to stop the pears from browning.

Lightly dust a clean work surface with a little flour and roll out the pastry into a large round about 35-cm wide. Transfer the rolled-out pastry to the lined baking tray and spoon over the chilled frangipane, leaving a 7-cm clear border all the way round. Top with the sliced pears, fanning out the quarters as you arrange them on the frangipane.

Working around the edges of the pastry, fold the border up and inwards to make a crust, folding or pleating the pastry when necessary. Do not worry about this looking messy. Brush the pastry edges with the egg white and sprinkle some caster sugar over both the pears and pastry.

Bake the galette in the oven for 45–50 minutes or until the pastry is golden and the frangipane has puffed slightly. Allow to cool.

When ready to serve, dust the galette with icing sugar. Serve slices of the galette with scoops of vanilla ice cream, if you like.

Do aheads

It is important that the pastry is cold, so I tend to make it the night before when time allows.

Chocolate marmalade tart

I think of this tart as a grown-up, dinner party-appropriate interpretation of a Jaffa cake. With a layer of amber marmalade running between the crisp pastry and rich chocolate filling, it looks wonderfully impressive when sliced and gives the impression that it requires a lot more effort to make than it really does. The filling is simple to prepare, only requiring a melt and a mix before being left to cool and set. If you are really pushed for time, you can use ready-rolled shortcrust pastry. I love to serve this tart with a dollop of crème fraîche.

Serves 8–10

Time 1 hour, plus at least 6 hours chilling and cooling

For the pastry

1 quantity of sweet shortcrust pastry (**p. 209**)

White spelt flour or white plain flour, to dust

For the filling

350g thick-set, orange marmalade (it must be a thick-set marmalade, not a runny one, to get a clean marmalade layer)

300ml double cream

30g caster sugar

Pinch of fine sea salt

300g dark chocolate (70% cocoa), roughly chopped

To serve

Crème fraîche (optional)

You wil also l need a 23-cm loose-based, fluted tart tin.

First, make the pastry following the instructions on page 209.

Lightly dust a clean work surface with a little flour and roll out the pastry into a round about 5-cm wider than a 23-cm loose-based, fluted tart tin. Line the tart tin with the pastry. Trim any excess pastry overhanging the edges of the tin and place it in the fridge to chill for 1 hour.

Preheat the oven to 180°C fan.

Line the chilled pastry case with parchment paper and fill it with ceramic baking beans. Bake the pastry case in the oven for 20 minutes. Remove the parchment paper and beans and bake for a further 15–20 minutes until golden. (The tart will not go back in the oven after this point, so make sure the pastry is fully cooked with a toasty golden colour at this point.) Allow the tart case to cool completely in the tin.

In a saucepan set over a low heat, warm the marmalade until it is in a liquid state. Strain through a sieve to remove any lumps. Re-weigh the marmalade – you should have about 250g left, but if not, melt a little more and repeat the sieving process. Pour the strained marmalade into your cooled tart case and allow it to set in the fridge.

Place the cream, sugar and salt in a saucepan set over a medium heat. Stir to help the sugar dissolve and allow it all to just come to a simmer. Immediately remove the pan from the heat, then stir through the chocolate until melted and smooth. Pour the chocolate mixture into the tart case over the marmalade layer. Chill in the fridge for at least 2 hours.

Before serving, allow the tart to sit at room temperature for 10 minutes. Serve with crème fraîche, if you like.

Do aheads

The baked pastry case can be made a day ahead, as can the entire tart. It will keep well in the fridge for up to 4 days, too.

Campari and blood orange jelly

I love a retro dinner-party pudding and there is nothing more retro than a jelly. Blood oranges are in season from December to late April when the weather in England can be quite gloomy. Vibrant red with a comical wobble, this jelly is the perfect tonic to winter weather. The bitter tartness of Campari is paired with sweet, juicy blood oranges. Don't worry if you cannot find fresh blood oranges – bottled juice is just as good and is sometimes more readily available. You can also, of course, just use regular oranges. I should add that this is quite boozy, which makes it the perfect after-dinner pudding.

Serves 8

Time 15–25 minutes, plus at least 6 hours chilling

500ml freshly squeezed blood orange juice or orange juice (from about 10 oranges, or you can use bottled juice)

200ml warm water

150g caster sugar

2 x 12g sachets of gelatine powder

300ml Campari

To serve

Whipped double cream or ice cream (optional)

You will also need a 1-litre jelly mould (I use a plastic one).

Very lightly oil your 1-litre jelly mould with a neutral oil such as sunflower oil. You don't have to do this but I find it helps the jelly release from the mould.

If using fresh oranges, squeeze the juice and then pass it through a sieve into a large bowl to remove any pulp or pips.

Place the warm water and sugar in a large saucepan set over a low heat. Gently whisk until all the grains of sugar have dissolved.

Remove from the heat and sprinkle the gelatine powder over the surface of the sugary water and whisk until dissolved. If any small lumps of gelatine remain, pass the mixture through a sieve.

Pour the orange juice and Campari into the pan with the gelatine mixture and stir to combine.

Pour the jelly mixture into your 1-litre jelly mould. Place the jelly in the fridge to chill for at least 6 hours (or overnight) until set.

Fill a bowl with warm (but not boiling) water. Remove the jelly from the fridge and dip the mould in the water for just 10 seconds, then carefully invert the jelly onto a plate. Serve with loosely whipped cream or ice cream, if you like.

Molten chocolate skillet brownie

This is a gloriously chocolatey pudding which is excellent for any occasion. The centre becomes molten and almost lava-like once baked, and is best enjoyed with some good vanilla ice cream (or try it with the No-churn Miso Caramel Pecan Ice Cream on page 166). Cooking it in a cast iron skillet pan means it will stay warmer and molten for longer, but if you don't have one, just use a cake tin.

Serves 6–8
Time 45 minutes

175g butter (plus extra to grease)
150g dark chocolate (70% cocoa), broken into pieces
100g plain flour
40g unsweetened cocoa powder
Pinch of fine sea salt
200g caster sugar
100g light soft brown sugar
3 large eggs, beaten
275g dark chocolate (70% cocoa), roughly chopped
Coarse sea salt flakes, to sprinkle

To serve

Vanilla ice cream

You will also need a 25-cm cast iron skillet or a 25-cm round cake tin.

Preheat the oven to 180°C fan. Lightly grease a 25-cm cast iron skillet or line a 25-cm round cake tin with parchment paper.

Melt the butter and broken-up dark chocolate in a heat-proof bowl set over a pan of simmering water until smooth and combined. Allow to cool slightly.

Whisk together the flour, cocoa powder and the pinch of salt in a separate bowl.

Whisk both sugars into the melted chocolate mixture, then whisk in the eggs. Fold in the flour mix, then fold in the chopped chocolate.

Pour the batter evenly into the cast iron skillet pan or cake tin and sprinkle over some sea salt flakes.

Bake in the oven for 20–25 minutes or until the top has set but the middle still wobbles. Allow it to rest for 5 minutes and then serve with ice cream.

Goes well with
- No-churn miso caramel pecan ice cream **p. 166**

Spiced ginger cake with whipped mascarpone

This cake is sticky and fudgy and rich. I think it tastes better the day after it is made, or even the following day, once the flavours have really had time to settle and the texture develops a good squidge. Make sure you keep the mascarpone and cream chilled until you are ready to make the frosting and take care not to overwhip them. If time allows, make the cake the day before, but be sure to wrap it tightly in beeswax wrap or cling film to prevent it from drying out. The cake will keep very well for about a week without the frosting, so if I am making it for myself, I will keep it that way and swap the frosting for a spoonful of crème fraîche whenever I have a slice.

Serves 12

Time 1 hour 30 minutes, plus chilling and cooling

For the dry ingredients

230g plain flour

½ tsp bicarbonate of soda

70g dark soft brown sugar

50g caster sugar

2 tsp ground ginger

2 tsp ground cinnamon (plus optional extra to dust)

2 tsp mixed spice

¼ tsp freshly grated nutmeg

For the wet ingredients

175ml sunflower oil

200g golden syrup

150g black treacle

1 tsp vanilla extract

2 large eggs

250ml semi-skimmed milk

For the whipped mascarpone frosting

250g mascarpone, chilled

100g icing sugar

300ml double cream, chilled

You will also need a 20-cm springform cake tin.

Do aheads

I think this cake tastes even better a day or two after it is made when the flavours have had time to settle, so I always make it the day before I intend to serve it.

Preheat the oven to 170°C fan and line the base and sides of a 20-cm springform cake tin with parchment paper.

In a large mixing bowl, whisk together all the dry ingredients until well combined.

In a medium bowl, whisk together the sunflower oil, golden syrup, black treacle and vanilla extract until well combined. One by one, beat the eggs into the oil mixture, followed by the milk.

Pour the combined wet ingredients into the combined dry ingredients and whisk until smooth.

Scrape the cake batter into the lined cake tin and spread evenly.

Bake the cake in the oven for 50–60 minutes or until the cake is springy to the touch and a skewer or cocktail stick inserted into the centre comes out clean. If the surface of the cake has cracked slightly, do not worry – it will settle. Allow the cake to cool in the tin for 15 minutes, then remove the sides of the tin and leave to cool completely. Once cool, remove from the tin base and tightly wrap the cake in beeswax wrap or cling film until ready to serve.

Make sure both the mascarpone and double cream are well chilled before making the frosting. To make the frosting, place the mascarpone in a large bowl and sift in the icing sugar. Using a silicone spatula or wooden spoon, work the two together until just combined, being careful not to overmix.

Pour the cream into the mascarpone. Using a handheld balloon whisk (not an electric one), whip the mascarpone and cream just until soft, droopy peaks form, taking care not to over whip.

Unwrap the cake, then spoon the frosting over the top and swirl the surface into rough peaks. Dust the cake with a little extra ground cinnamon, if you like.

BETTER BASICS

FENNEL SEED VINAIGRETTE
186

TAHINI DRESSING
187

GREEN TAHINI
188

SESAME MISO DRESSING
189

LABNEH
190

WHIPPED FETA
192

WHIPPED TAHINI YOGURT
193

MAYONNAISE
194

SALSA VERDE, TWO WAYS
196

CONFIT GARLIC
197

WHOLEGRAIN YOGURT FLATBREADS
199

SIMPLE SODA BREAD
200

WHOLEGRAIN FOCACCIA
202

NO-KNEAD SPELT LOAF
204

COMPOUND BUTTERS
205

SEEDED SPELT CRACKERS
206

BASIC SHORTCRUST PASTRY
208

I find it is often the simplest things that take a meal from bland to brilliant. It could be as basic as a handful of herbs, a squeeze of fresh lemon or a quick dressing tossed through right at the end. This is the chapter dedicated to these types of recipes. None of them are complicated but each of them can be used in or with a variety of ways and dishes. You can enjoy a bowl of whipped feta simply drizzled with some olive oil to be swooshed up with some seeded crackers or fluffy flatbreads, or you can use it to elevate some roasted vegetables to give them a bit more oomph. These are basic recipes but they are also often the elements that make things better.

Fennel seed vinaigrette

This is my go-to salad dressing that makes even the saddest lettuce leaf more exciting. It is equally good tossed through some shredded kale or finely sliced fennel. I also love to add it to a combination of grated carrot and shredded red cabbage to make a simple winter slaw.

The quantities given here make enough dressing for one salad, however, it will keep at room temperature well for up to a week so you can increase the amounts to make more, if you like.

Makes enough for 1 salad
Time 10 minutes

1 tsp fennel seeds
3 tbsp olive oil
1 tbsp sherry vinegar or moscatel vinegar
1 tsp runny honey
Large pinch of sea salt

In a dry frying pan set over a gentle heat, lightly toast the fennel seeds for about 3 minutes until they begin to smell fragrant.

Transfer to a pestle and mortar and gently crush. (You can also use a small bowl and the base of a spice jar or end of a rolling pin for this.)

In a small bowl or jar, combine the olive oil, vinegar, honey and salt. Whisk or shake in the crushed toasted fennel seeds.

Goes well with

- This is a brilliant way to bring a bit more oomph to a green salad; some shaved parmesan added in is delicious, too
- Chicory and pear seeded salad, in the place of the existing dressing **p. 32**
- Tossed into some grated carrot and red cabbage as a simple winter slaw. Any chopped, toasted nuts are an excellent addition.

Tahini dressing

I mostly make this creamy dressing to toss through any leftover grilled vegetables or some shredded hardy greens, such as kale or cavolo nero. It is also very good on some classic green leaves, such as romaine or baby gem.

Makes enough for 1 salad
Time 5 minutes

3 tbsp tahini
3 tbsp olive oil
1 garlic clove, finely grated
1 tbsp sherry vinegar
Juice of ½ lemon
Large pinch of sea salt

Add the tahini, olive oil, garlic, vinegar and lemon juice to a small bowl or jar. Whisk or shake together. Do not worry if the dressing seizes.

Slowly add a little cold water (about 100–150ml) in a steady stream, whisking continuously, until the dressing reaches the consistency of double cream. Add a good pinch of salt. Taste to check the seasoning, adding more lemon juice or salt as needed.

Do aheads

The dressing can be made and stored in the fridge for up to a week.

Goes well with

- Winter greens with almonds and figs (**p. 37**), instead of the anchovy dressing
- Some shredded or grated vegetables. Try it as an alternative dressing in the carrot and coriander salad (**p. 24**) or with some shredded raw cabbage
- I often throw this on some simple roasted or steamed veg. It is particularly good on broccoli or cauliflower florets tossed in olive oil and salt and roasted in an oven set to 200°C fan for 15–20 minutes until slightly charred

Green tahini

I love green tahini and could eat it with almost anything. It is very good with grilled meat or vegetables (see Herby Meatballs with Green Tahini on page 60 and Grilled Aubergines with Green Tahini on page 134), but I also love to spoon it over cooked eggs or even just a simple plate of sliced tomatoes. It is packed full of flavour and an excellent accompaniment to perk up any leftovers.

Makes enough for 1 salad
Time 10 minutes

Large bunch of parsley (about 100g)
Small bunch of mint (about 25g)
1 garlic clove, finely grated
1 green bird's eye chilli, roughly chopped
Juice of 1 lemon
3 tbsp tahini
1 tsp ground coriander
Large pinch of coarse sea salt flakes

Tear the leafy parts from the bunch of parsley. Pick the leaves from the sprigs of mint.

Place the leafy herbs in a high-speed blender (I use a Nutribullet) with the remaining ingredients and 50ml of cold water. If you're sensitive to heat, you can remove the seeds from the chilli first. Pulse the mixture roughly six times to encourage the herbs to break down. Once the herbs have begun to collapse, blitz continuously until the mixture is smooth and creamy. If you need to add more water (up to an extra 50ml) to achieve your preferred consistency, do so now.

Taste to check the seasoning, adjusting with more lemon juice or salt as needed.

Do aheads

This dressing will keep well in the fridge for up to 3 days so you can increase the amounts to make more.

Goes well with

- Herby meatballs with green tahini **p. 60**
- Grilled aubergines with green tahini **p. 134**
- Alongside the potato rösti with fried eggs and soft herbs **p. 62**
- This is also excellent alongside some BBQ'd meat (particularly chicken or lamb)
- You could also enjoy it with some toast and a crispy fried or soft-boiled egg

Sesame miso dressing

This dressing is particularly good with crunchy raw veg. It is the dressing I turn to most during the summer months, tossing it through a medley of carrots, sugar snaps, cabbage, broccoli or even just some grated carrots on their own.

Makes enough dressing for 1 salad
Time 5 minutes

1 tbsp white miso paste (if using brown rice miso paste, you may want to add more honey)
4 tbsp toasted sesame oil
Juice of ½ lime
1 tbsp runny honey
1 garlic clove, finely grated
Thumb-sized piece of fresh ginger, peeled and finely grated

In a small bowl or jar, combine all the ingredients for the dressing. Whisk with a fork or shake until smooth.

Do aheads
This dressing will keep well in the fridge for up to a week so you can increase the amounts to make more.

Goes well with
- Carrot and coriander salad, as an alternative to the dressing p. 24
- Grilled aubergines with green tahini, in the place of the green tahini p. 134
- Some shredded hardy greens such as kale or cavolo nero
- This is also very good as a sticky glaze for roasted aubergines. I like to halve my aubergines and criss-cross the fleshy centre with a knife, before rubbing them in olive oil and roasting them on a parchment paper-lined baking tray in an oven set to 200°C fan for about 30 minutes, until cooked through and golden. Spread the dressing over the cooked aubergines and return to the oven for 8–10 minutes until sticky and golden

Labneh

Labneh is something that often appears on restaurant menus and so we perhaps assume it is fairly complicated to make. In reality, it couldn't be easier. Labneh is made simply by hanging yogurt in a fine-mesh cloth to allow the liquid whey to drain out, until you are left with a soft cheese that is wonderfully creamy and smooth. You can also enjoy it as a pudding, omitting the salt and leaving it fresh and tangy, or stirring through some icing sugar before serving with some baked fruit (such as the Baked Figs and Plums with Whipped Honey Yogurt and Amaretti on page 172).

Makes 500g, enough for 6
Time 10 minutes hands-on time, plus up to 12 hours resting

Pinch of fine sea salt
500g full-fat Greek yogurt

The night before you intend to eat the labneh, stir the salt through the yogurt.

Rest a sieve over a bowl and line it with a muslin cloth or a jam bag (you can even use a clean pair of tights). Spoon the yogurt into the centre of the cloth or bag. Bring up the four corners of the muslin cloth or bag and secure them at the top with string or an elastic band to make a bag.

Suspend the bag over the bowl to allow the whey to drain from the yogurt. In the winter when my kitchen is cold enough, I hang the bag on the handle of a wall cupboard suspended over the bowl on my kitchen counter and leave it there overnight. During the warmer months, it is best to let the yogurt drain inside the fridge. Let the yogurt hang for at least 12 hours – the longer you leave the labneh, the thicker and firmer it will become.

Once the labneh has hung sufficiently to achieve your preferred texture, discard the liquid whey in the bowl. Give the labneh a gentle stir to soften slightly, then serve.

Do aheads

The labneh will keep in an airtight container for up to 5 days in the fridge.

Goes well with

- Harissa sesame carrots with labneh **p. 95**
- Roasted beetroot with whipped feta and green chilli salsa (**p. 116**, as an alternative to the whipped feta)
- Potato rösti with fried eggs and soft herbs **p. 62**
- Crackers or flatbreads and a drizzle of olive oil and sprinkle of za'atar as a snack (see seeded spelt crackers **p. 206** and wholegrain flatbreads **p. 199**)
- On toast with roasted or confit vegetables (see fennel, shallot, tomato and garlic confit with burrata **p. 108**)
- On toast with confit garlic and a drizzle of honey (see confit garlic **p. 197**)

Whipped feta

I often use whipped feta as a way of dressing up some simple roasted vegetables. It instantly elevates them from being just a side to the star of the table (see Roasted Beetroot with Whipped Feta and Green Chilli Salsa on page 116). Whipped feta also makes a very good dip if you are in need of something simple to enjoy with drinks or to offer to friends as a snack. If serving it as a dip, I finish it with a drizzle of good olive oil and some za'atar or even a little grated lemon zest.

Makes 350g, enough for 6
Time 10 minutes

200g feta
150g full-fat Greek yogurt
Juice of ½ lemon

Crumble the feta into a food processor and pulse to break the cheese down.

Add the yogurt and lemon juice, then blitz until smooth. Chill until ready to serve.

Do aheads
This will keep for up to 5 days in the fridge in an airtight container.

Goes well with
- Roasted beetroot with whipped feta and green chilli salsa **p. 116**
- Grilled sugar snap peas with lemony ricotta, in the place of the ricotta **p. 133**
- Harissa sesame carrots with labneh, in the place of the labneh **p. 95**
- Potato rösti with fried eggs and soft herbs **p. 62**
- Crackers or flatbreads and a drizzle of olive oil and sprinkle of za'atar as a snack (see seeded spelt crackers **p. 206** and wholegrain flatbreads **p. 199**)
- On toast with roasted or confit vegetables (see fennel, shallot, tomato and garlic confit with burrata **p. 108**)
- On toast with confit garlic and a drizzle of honey (see confit garlic **p. 197**)

Whipped tahini yogurt

This whipped tahini yogurt makes a very good base for some grilled or roasted vegetables, but it is just as delicious with BBQ'd meats. I might marinate the meat with a bit of chilli before cooking and then serve the whipped tahini yogurt alongside to offset the heat.

Makes enough for 4–6 people
Time 10 minutes

300g full-fat Greek yogurt
1 tbsp tahini
½ garlic clove, finely grated
Juice of ½ lemon
Pinch of salt

Combine all the ingredients in a bowl. Whisk everything together (by hand) until thick and creamy. Chill until ready to serve.

Do aheads
This will keep for up to 5 days in the fridge in an airtight container.

Goes well with
- Grilled sugar snap peas with lemony ricotta, in the place of the ricotta **p. 133**
- Harissa sesame carrots with labneh, in the place of the labneh **p. 95**
- Grilled aubergines with green tahini, in the place of the green tahini **p. 134**
- Flatbreads (see wholegrain flatbreads **p. 199**)
- As a cooling condiment to some BBQ'd chicken or vegetables

Mayonnaise

Homemade mayonnaise is one of those things that always seems far more impressive than it really is but is undeniably worth it. These are my favourite variations all of which can be made with a handheld whisk or with a food processor. These will all keep for up to 3 days in the fridge.

Classic

Makes 400g
Takes 10 minutes

2 large egg yolks
1 heaped tsp Dijon mustard
Juice of ½ lemon (about 2 tbsp juice)
Good pinch of fine sea salt
150ml olive oil
150ml sunflower oil (or use 300ml light olive oil in place of the two oils)

Place the egg yolks, mustard, lemon juice and salt into a medium-sized bowl and whisk to combine.

Combine the olive oil and sunflower oil in a jug and then very slowly drizzle it into the yolks mixture, whisking continuously as you do. Keep whisking and adding the oil slowly until you have a thick, glossy mayonnaise. You may not need to use all of the oil.

Alternatively, add the egg yolks, mustard, lemon juice and salt to a food processor. Pulse to combine, then add the oil slowly while the machine runs.

Taste to season, adjusting the salt and lemon juice as necessary.

Goes well with

- Crispy potatoes (cooked as per the recipe on page 96)
- Springtime fritters **p. 49**
- Courgette, anchovy and lemon fritti **p. 57**

Aioli

Makes 400g
Takes 10 minutes

2 large egg yolks
1 heaped tsp Dijon mustard
Juice of ½ lemon (about 2 tbsp juice)
1 fat garlic clove, finely grated or crushed
Good pinch of fine sea salt
150ml olive oil
150ml sunflower oil (or use 300ml light olive oil in place of the two oils)

Place the egg yolks, mustard, lemon juice, garlic and salt into a medium-sized bowl and whisk to combine.

Combine the olive oil and sunflower oil in a jug and then very slowly drizzle it into the yolks mixture, whisking continuously as you do. Keep whisking and adding the oil slowly until you have a thick, glossy mayonnaise. You may not need to use all of the oil.

Alternatively, add the egg yolks, mustard, lemon juice, garlic and salt to a food processor. Pulse to combine, then add the oil slowly while the machine runs.

Taste to season, adjusting the salt and lemon the as necessary.

Goes well with

- Crispy potatoes (cooked as per the recipe on page 96)
- I love this with the baked chicken with La Ratte potatoes and romesco (**p. 111**) for an additional garlicky hit
- It's also very good enjoyed simply with some fresh crunchy raw vegetables such as radishes and baby carrots

Saffron mayonnaise

Makes 400g
Takes 15 minutes

Pinch of saffron
1 tbsp boiling water
2 large egg yolks
1 heaped tsp Dijon mustard
1 tsp white wine vinegar
Good pinch of fine sea salt
150ml olive oil
150ml sunflower oil (or use 300ml light olive oil in place of the two oils)

Steep the saffron in the boiling water, crushing it a little between your fingers as you add it. Allow it to sit for 5 minutes and let it come to room temperature.

Place the egg yolks, mustard, vinegar and salt into a medium-sized bowl and whisk to combine.

Combine the olive oil and sunflower oil in a jug and then very slowly drizzle it into the yolks mixture, whisking continuously as you do. Once the mayonnaise has started to thicken and emulsify, add half the saffron water, allowing the saffron strands to go with it, drizzling it in slowly as you did the oil.

Repeat this step, adding a little more oil, the remaining saffron water and then the remaining oil. Adjust the seasoning as necessary. You may need a little more or a little less oil.

Alternatively, add the egg yolks, mustard, vinegar and salt to a food processor. Pulse to combine, then slowly add about one-quarter of the oil, followed by half the saffron water and then alternate between the remaining oil and saffron water, adding both slowly while the machine runs.

Taste to season, adjusting the salt and vinegar as necessary.

Goes well with

- This is particularly good with the springtime fritters **p. 49**
- Courgette, anchovy and lemon fritti **p. 57**
- Baked salmon with blood orange and chilli **p. 122**

Salsa verde, two ways

Salsa verde is probably the accompaniment that I lean on most of all. It is incredibly versatile and pairs well with chicken, fish, vegetables or even as a salad dressing (see Salsa Verde Salad on page 25). I wanted to give two ways of making it – chopped or blitzed – as I vary the way I make it when at home. Sometimes it comes down to how much time I have, but on other occasions it is because a creamier blitzed sauce works better for a particular dish as opposed to a more textured chopped one.

Makes enough for 6
Time 10–15 minutes

Large bunch of parsley (about 100g), leaves torn

Medium bunch of mint (about 50g), leaves picked

Medium bunch of tarragon or basil (about 50g)

2 tbsp capers, rinsed and drained

6 tinned anchovy fillets, drained

1 large garlic clove, finely chopped or grated

1 heaped tsp Dijon mustard

2 tbsp red wine vinegar

Juice of ½ lemon (or more to taste)

Pinch of salt

6 tbsp olive oil (plus extra as needed)

Chopped

Chop the herbs, capers and anchovies as coarsely or as finely as you wish. Add the garlic, mustard, vinegar, lemon juice, salt and enough olive oil to achieve a spoonable consistency. Taste to check the seasoning, adjusting with more lemon juice or salt, as needed. It should be sharp and vibrant.

Blitzed

Place all the ingredients for the salsa verde in a high-speed blender (I use a Nutribullet). Pulse the mixture a few times to break the ingredients down. If they are resisting, add a little more olive oil. Once the herbs have begun to collapse, blitz continuously until the mixture is smooth. Taste to check the seasoning, adjusting with more lemon juice or salt, as needed. It should be sharp and vibrant.

Do aheads
This will keep in a jar in the fridge for up to 3 days.

Goes well with
- Salsa verde salad p. 25
- Potato rösti with fried eggs and soft herbs p. 62
- Crispy za'atar smashed potatoes p. 96
- Butterflied leg of lamb with red wine vinegar p. 146
- It's also very good alongside any BBQ'd chicken or vegetables
- I love leftovers stirred through pasta as a punchy green sauce, too
- Enjoy it spread onto toast and topped with some crumbled feta or a crispy fried egg, or both!

Confit garlic

It may seem tedious to peel two entire bulbs of garlic, but it is well worth it for confit garlic. You can peel less, if you like, but I find there is not much point in making only a small amount, and trust me, you will be wishing you had more once the confit garlic is finished. The garlic goes beautifully soft and jammy as it cooks, losing all of its astringency and becoming almost sweet. You will be left with a wonderfully flavoured oil, too, which must be kept and enjoyed for dipping, drizzling and dressings.

Makes 1 jam jar of confit garlic
Time 50 minutes

2 or more whole bulbs of garlic
Olive oil
2 rosemary sprigs or thyme sprigs

Break open the garlic bulbs and separate the individual cloves. Peel each garlic clove and place them in a small saucepan. Add enough olive oil to the pan to cover all the garlic, then add the rosemary or thyme sprigs.

Place the pan over the very lowest heat and slowly cook for 30–40 minutes or until the garlic cloves are soft and jammy. Keep an eye on the oil – if it begins to bubble, remove the pan from the heat temporarily until the bubbles subside and then return it to the heat.

When kept in an airtight container, the confit garlic can be stored in the fridge for up to 2 weeks.

Do aheads
The oil and the confit garlic can be stored in a clean jar in the fridge for up to 3 days.

Goes well with
There are so many ways that you can enjoy confit garlic. I confess to eating the cloves straight out of the jar, but I have listed below some of my favourite ways to serve it:

- Spooned over labneh **p. 190** and served with bread or seeded spelt crackers **p. 206**
- Smooshed onto toast with a fried egg
- Spooned over lemony ricotta **p. 133** on toast
- As a condiment with something crisp (such as potato rösti with fried eggs and soft herbs on page 62)
- Smooshed into salad dressings
- Tossed through steamed vegetables with olive oil
- Whisked into butter to spread onto wholegrain flatbreads **p. 199**
- Added to brothy stews and beans
- Use any remaining garlic-infused oil in dressings, on salads and vegetables

Wholegrain flatbreads

I make a batch of flatbreads whenever I have friends over for a BBQ. They cook quickly on the grill and are essential for mopping up saucy dressings or any other juicy bits. These wholegrain flatbreads are made in one bowl and require minimal resting time, which means you can make them with very little notice. What really makes them is the garlicky, herby melted butter brushed over each one as soon as they come off the grill or out of the pan.

Makes 6
Time 45 minutes–1 hour

For the flatbreads
200g wholegrain spelt flour (regular wholegrain flour works, too) (plus extra to dust)
4 tsp baking powder
Pinch of salt
200g natural yogurt

For the butter
50g butter
3 garlic cloves, crushed
1 tbsp finely chopped parsley leaves
1 tbsp finely chopped dill
1 tbsp finely chopped mint leaves
Pinch of salt

In a large bowl, whisk together the flour, baking powder and salt. Add the yogurt and, using your hands, bring everything together into a rough dough. Allow the dough to rest for about 10 minutes while you prepare the butter.

In a small saucepan, melt the butter with the crushed garlic. Turn off the heat and stir through the chopped herbs and salt. Set aside.

Divide the dough in half, then divide each half into three equal-sized pieces. On a lightly floured surface, roll out each piece to a round about 12-cm wide. Gently score the surface of each flatbread in the centre with a sharp knife – I make three slashes.

In a dry frying pan set over a medium-high heat, cook the flatbreads, one at a time, for 2–3 minutes on each side until lightly browned in places. Alternatively, cook the flatbreads on the BBQ over a medium heat for 2–3 minutes on each side. As they come off the heat, brush each flatbread with the garlic herb butter.

Goes well with
- Harissa sesame carrots with labneh **p. 95**
- Grilled aubergines with green tahini **p. 134**
- Spiced aubergine on cold garlic yogurt **p. 71**
- Whipped feta **p. 192**
- Labneh **p. 190**

Simple soda bread

Soda bread is the baking novice's secret to being a domestic goddess. You can make it from start to finish in an hour. There is no kneading and no rising involved. The messier the loaf, the better it is. I love it still warm from the oven with lots of butter, but I will often add dried fruit and nuts or sometimes herbs. I have made some suggestions for different variations below, following the basic soda bread recipe.

Serves 10
Time 1 hour

400g wholegrain spelt or wheat flour (plus extra to sprinkle)
50g rolled porridge oats (plus extra to sprinkle)
1 tsp bicarbonate of soda
1 tsp salt
500g full-fat natural yogurt

Preheat the oven to 200°C fan and line a baking tray with a sheet of parchment paper.

In a large bowl, whisk together the flour, oats, bicarbonate of soda and salt. Add the yogurt and, using your hands or a bench scraper, bring everything together into a scraggy, wet dough. (It will be messy.)

Shape the dough into a ball, as best you can. Add a little more flour, if needed, but the dough should be very sticky and wet. It doesn't need to be neat. Plop the dough onto the lined baking tray.

Using a large knife or bench scraper, mark a cross in the dough, bringing the knife or scraper about half or three-quarters of the way down. Sprinkle the dough with a little extra flour and a few more oats.

Bake the bread in the oven for 35–45 minutes. After 35 minutes, check the bread. When cooked, it should sound hollow-ish when tapped on the bottom. Remove from the oven and leave to cool on a wire rack.

When cool enough to handle, cut the soda bread into slices and serve.

The bread will keep wrapped or in an airtight container for a day or two, but I always think it tastes best the day it is made.

Fig and pecan soda bread

Ingredients as given for the simple soda bread, plus:
150g dates, stones removed and roughly chopped
80g pecans, roughly chopped

Toss the dates in a little flour to stop them from sticking together. Stir the chopped dates and pecans through the flour and oats mixture before adding the yogurt, then continue as instructed above.

Grana padano and rosemary soda bread

Ingredients as given for the simple soda bread, plus:
150g finely grated Grana Padano or Parmesan (plus extra to sprinkle)
2 tbsp finely chopped rosemary

Stir the grated cheese and chopped rosemary through the flour and oats mixture before adding the yogurt, then continue as instructed above. Sprinkle a little more grated cheese over the soda bread before baking.

Wholegrain focaccia

I went through a phase of vigilantly tending to my sourdough starter. On the weekends, I would make a sourdough focaccia, starting the process on Friday in order to bake it on Sunday. All that attentiveness went out the window once I had a baby. Still, I longed for the tangy flavour of my sourdough focaccia and wanted to find a way to create a similar taste, which was missing with most fast-action yeast recipes. This process is almost the same as the quicker methods for making focaccia, except the dough rests in the fridge overnight for a slower prove, echoing the way you would make a sourdough bread. Adding salt slows down the fermentation process even further which, together with the wholegrain flour, brings a more complex, nutty flavour to the focaccia.

Serves 10

Time 1 hour, plus at least 15 hours resting

400g strong white bread flour

100g wholegrain flour

7g fast-action dried yeast

10g fine sea salt

500ml lukewarm water

Olive oil

Small bunch of rosemary (about 25g)

Coarse sea salt flakes

You will also need a 25-cm square deep baking tin.

The day before, make the dough. In a large bowl, whisk together the flours, yeast and salt.

Make a well in the flour and pour in the water. Using a silicone spatula or bench scraper, bring the dough together, pulling the flour in from the edges, until you have a very wet dough.

Pour about 2 tablespoons of olive oil into your hands over the dough. Run your oiled hands over the dough, then very lightly tuck the edges down, allowing the oil to dribble over so that the entire dough is covered in a layer of oil. Cover the oiled dough with cling film and place in the fridge to rest for 12–16 hours.

In the morning, line the base and sides of a 25-cm square deep baking tin with parchment paper, leaving some excess paper overhanging the top edges of the tin. Generously oil the paper, including the sides.

Remove the dough from the fridge and unwrap it. With oiled hands, gently pull it away from the sides of the bowl and transfer the dough to the oiled lined baking tin. Leave the dough somewhere warm, uncovered, to rest for 3–4 hours or until it has relaxed into the shape of the tin and increased in size.

When bubbles are beginning to form, the dough is nearly ready. Preheat the oven to 225°C fan.

Strip the leaves from the rosemary sprigs, add them to a small bowl and coat them in a tablespoon of olive oil. (This will prevent the rosemary leaves from burning.)

Drizzle the focaccia in the tin with a generous amount of olive oil and scatter over the rosemary leaves. Using your fingers, push dimples into the dough by pressing all the way down to the base of the tin. Sprinkle generously with sea salt flakes.

Bake the focaccia in the oven for 25 minutes or until golden.

Goes well with

- Pan-fried courgettes with mozzarella and pistachio butter **p. 54**
- Baked ricotta with romano peppers **p. 102**
- Fennel, shallot, tomato and garlic confit with burrata **p. 108**

As soon as the focaccia comes out of the oven, cover it with a clean tea towel and leave for 15 minutes. (This ensures the crust stays soft and bubbly.)

Using the overhanging parchment paper, lift the focaccia out of the tin and transfer to a wire rack to cool completely, then serve.

No-knead spelt loaf

I make this loaf at least once a month. I tend to slice it up immediately and freeze it as it keeps beautifully when frozen. I use wholegrain spelt flour which is wholesome and hearty, and gives the loaf a nuttiness, too. I probably eat it most with crunchy peanut butter, but it is good on the side of almost every dish or as a base for any scooped-up leftovers.

Makes 1 loaf, or 10–12 slices
Time 1 hour 15 minutes

500g wholegrain spelt flour
1 tsp baking powder
1 tsp bicarbonate of soda
1 tsp salt
530ml lukewarm water
Handful of mixed seeds of choice

You will also need a 900-g loaf tin.

Preheat the oven to 180°C fan and line a 900-g loaf tin with parchment paper.

In a large bowl, whisk together the flour, baking powder, bicarbonate of soda and salt. Add the lukewarm water and mix everything together until just combined.

Pour the dough into the lined loaf tin and scatter the mixed seeds over the top.

Bake the bread in the oven for 1 hour. The bread should have achieved a generous rise in the oven with a pale brown colour. Use the baking parchment to lift the loaf from the tin and tap the bottom – it should sound hollow. Remove from the oven and leave on a wire rack to cool. Serve in slices.

The bread will keep well when frozen in slices. I let it sit in the toaster for about 10 minutes to defrost a bit before toasting.

Goes well with
- This is my go-to loaf, so I probably eat it most with crunchy peanut butter, but it is an excellent all-rounder
- For something a little more special, I love to serve this with a compound butter such as the ones you'll find opposite

Compound butters

Makes about 300g
Takes 10 minutes

I love the flexibility of compound butters and how much flavour they can bring. The flavour combinations are endless but these are perhaps my most used. I love them with some warm bread, but they are also very good thrown onto some grilled meat, fish or vegetables and even stirred through hot pasta.

Rosemary chilli and walnut

30g walnuts

250g unsalted butter, soft at room temperature

3 tablespoons rosemary leaves, finely chopped

Pinch of Aleppo pepper flakes

Good pinch of flaky sea salt

Preheat the oven to 180°C and bake the nuts on a baking tray for 8–10 minutes. Allow them to cool then roughly chop.

Combine the remaining ingredients in a bowl and bring together using a whisk or fork.

Transfer to a sheet of parchment paper and shape into roughly a 12-cm long log shape. Roll the parchment paper to encase the butter, twisting each side as though you were creating a giant sweet wrapper.

Chill the butter in the fridge until firm.

Caper lemon garlic butter

250g unsalted butter, soft at room temperature

2 tablespoons capers, rinsed, drained and roughly chopped

Grated zest of 1 unwaxed lemon, plus 1 tbsp juice

1 fat garlic clove, finely grated or crushed

Good pinch of flaky sea salt

Combine all the ingredients in a bowl and bring together using a whisk or fork.

Sesame honey miso butter

250g unsalted butter, soft at room temperature

1 heaped tablespoon white miso paste

1 tbsp toasted sesame oil

1 tbsp runny honey

½ garlic clove, finely grated or crushed

Small pinch of flaky sea salt

About 2–3 tbsp toasted sesame seeds

Either combine all the ingredients following the method as above or, if you like, combine all the ingredients apart from the sesame seeds and then roll the butter in the sesame seeds before chilling so that the roll is coated in the seeds.

Seeded spelt crackers

There are lots of good crackers available in the shops, but I love the rustic nature of these spelt ones. This recipe makes two large sheets of crackers, which are then broken up into irregular shapes. These crackers are very good for general snacking or enjoying with dips, plus they look excellent on a cheeseboard.

Makes 2 large sheets of crackers
Time 1 hour

275g white spelt flour (plus extra to dust)
2 tbsp toasted white sesame seeds
2 tbsp black sesame seeds
1 tbsp nigella seeds
2 tsp coarse sea salt flakes (plus extra to finish)
100ml olive oil (plus extra to brush)

Preheat the oven to 170°C fan and line two baking sheets with parchment paper or silicone baking mats.

Place the flour, both lots of sesame seeds, the nigella seeds and salt flakes in a food processor. Pulse briefly to combine. Add the olive oil along with 150ml of cold water, then pulse until the mixture just comes together to form a wet dough.

Divide the dough in half. On a lightly floured surface, roll out each piece to a thickness of 2-mm and transfer to the lined baking sheets. Alternatively, roll out the dough directly onto the lightly floured parchment paper or silicone baking mats and then lift everything onto the baking sheets.

Brush the dough with olive oil, prick the surface all over with a fork and then sprinkle with a generous amount of sea salt flakes.

Bake the crackers in the oven for 30–40 minutes or until crisp, turning the baking sheets halfway through to ensure even cooking. Allow the crackers to cool on the baking sheets before snapping the sheets into large irregular pieces.

Goes well with
- Grilled sugar snap peas with lemony ricotta **p. 133**
- Labneh **p. 190**
- Spiced aubergine on cold garlic yogurt **p. 71**
- Hummus or as part of a cheeseboard

Basic shortcrust pastry

Makes enough for 23-cm 1 tart or galette
Time 15 minutes, plus at least 2 hours chilling

Savoury shortcrust pastry

250g white spelt flour or white plain flour
Pinch of fine sea salt
140g unsalted butter, cold and cut into cubes
1 large egg, lightly beaten
1–2 tsp ice-cold water

I make my pastry in a food processor, which could not be simpler, but I have included instructions for how to do this by hand as well. Homemade pastry makes all the difference to a dish and so it is well worth it. I cannot stress how important it is to chill your dough. If time allows, I will always make my pastry the night before so that it is sufficiently chilled. Not only is pastry easier to handle when properly chilled, it also prevents it from releasing its fats too quickly and shrinking in the oven.

Place the flour and salt in the bowl of a food processor and pulse briefly to combine. Add the cold butter and blitz again until the mixture resembles breadcrumbs. Next, add the beaten egg and just 1 teaspoon of the ice-cold water, then pulse again until the mixture starts to come together as a dough. Only add the remaining ice-cold water if needed.

Alternatively, to make the pastry by hand, whisk together the flour and salt in a large bowl. Rub in the cold butter with your fingertips until the mixture resembles breadcrumbs. Next, add the beaten egg and just 1 teaspoon of the ice-cold water, then bring the dough together with your hands. Only add the remaining ice-cold water if needed.

Without handling it too much, shape the dough into a flat disc, wrap it tightly in cling film and place in the fridge to chill for at least 2 hours. (If short on time, you can put it in the freezer for 20 minutes.)

Use the pastry dough as directed in the recipe.

Sweet shortcrust pastry

This is very similar to the savoury pastry, but it is slightly more delicate and works well for sweeter recipes.

200g white spelt flour or white plain flour
30g icing sugar
Pinch of fine sea salt
130g butter, cold and cut into cubes
1 large egg yolk (reserve the egg white for an egg wash if making a galette)
2 tbsp ice-cold water

Place the flour, sugar and salt in the bowl of a food processor and pulse briefly to combine. Add the cold butter and pulse again until the mixture resembles breadcrumbs. Next, add the egg yolk and ice-cold water and pulse again until the mixture starts to come together as a dough.

Alternatively, to make the pastry by hand, whisk together the flour, sugar and salt in a large bowl. Rub in the cold butter with your fingertips until the mixture resembles breadcrumbs. Next, add the egg yolk and ice-cold water, then bring the dough together with your hands.

Without handling it too much, shape the dough into a flat disc, wrap it tightly in cling film and place in the fridge to chill for at least 2 hours. (If short on time, you can put it in the freezer for 20 minutes, then use as required.)

Use the pastry dough as directed in the recipe.

A MENU FOR...

Whatever the scenario, I will be making dinner. Even if dinner means leftover chicken and cold potatoes tossed into a salad and jazzed up with a good dressing. I find cooking, both for myself and for others, the easiest way to find a sense of grounding joy but I know there are days when you have to search a little harder for inspiration as to what to cook. I wanted to share some of my favourite combinations of recipes for those special and unspecial occasions, and everything in between.

A CELEBRATION IN SPRING

Springtime fritters
49

Asparagus and green bean mimosa salad
15

Chicken with saffron and chickpeas
104

Pistachio tiramisu
161

A SLOW SUNDAY (LUNCH)

Cider-braised chicken with apples
127

Fennel, thyme and crème fraîche gratin
124

Cavolo nero with anchovy, chilli and hazelnuts
63

Spiced ginger cake with whipped mascarpone
181

AN EASY SATURDAY

Hake puttanesca
105

New potatoes with anchovy chive butter
77

Artichoke, fennel and parmesan salad
16

Pear and hazelnut frangipane galette
175

SOMETHING QUICK AND EASY ON THE SOFA

Pan-fried chicken with chilli, tomatoes and mint
58

Or

Soft courgettes with chickpeas, lemon and mint
78

Winter greens with almonds and figs
37

THE LAST-MINUTE DINNER PARTY

Crispy chicken thighs with lemon and pink peppercorns
119

New potatoes with anchovy chive butter
77

Salsa verde salad
25

Baked figs and plums with whipped honey yogurt and amaretti
172

WHEN THE SUN IS SHINING

Tomato salad
41

Wholegrain flatbreads
199

Stuffed squid with tomatoes and feta
144

Harissa honey chicken wings
151

Fruit and nut rice
87

Strawberry flapjack tart
157

WHEN YOU WANT TO CELEBRATE

Baked salmon with blood orange and chilli
122

Crispy za'atar smashed potatoes
96

Za'atar cabbage, fennel, apple slaw
40

Flourless chocolate meringue cake
158

JUST THE TWO OF YOU ♥

Pan-fried seabass with olive salsa
64

Winter greens with almonds and figs
37

Chocolate marmalade tart
176

ACKNOWLEDGEMENTS

I have tried my very best to keep things both simple and brief so far but this is going to be a long list (sorry!!). There are so many people to whom I will be forever grateful. I still can't quite believe I am here, writing this book. It has been a dream for so long and I couldn't have done it on my own.

First of all, thank you to you, for buying this book. This would not have happened without you. Thank you for supporting me, for reading my writing and cooking my recipes. The novelty of seeing you cook them in your own kitchen will never ever get old. Thank you to those who sent messages telling me you cooked the chicken for your Granny and that she loved it, or that you turn to my recipes because they are simple and easy to follow. It's you who helped me believe that there was a place for this book.

Thank you to my brilliant, kind and persistent agent Sabhbh Curran at Curtis Brown. It was a roller coaster of a ride but one that I never felt abandoned on. Thank you for holding my hand throughout it all, for listening to me and quietening my anxieties. Thank you for your constant support and excitement even when things were uncertain. Thank you for believing in me and believing in this. Woo! We did it.

A huge thank you to Celia Palazzo and the entire Ebury team. Celia, this book wouldn't be what it is now without your vision. Thank you for shaping it into what it is, and for guiding me and encouraging me to have faith in the simplicity of my ideas. It is a better book because of you.

Thank you to Florence Blair who I am lucky enough to have worked with on jobs of various shapes and sizes but who I am also lucky enough to call a friend. It is an oddly scary thing handing your recipes over to someone else to take them from the page to the plate, but I am quite certain there is no safer pair of hands that could have brought this book to life than yours. I trust your instinct entirely and you made everything look better than I could have imagined. Thank you also for the walks around London Fields when this book felt like a faraway dream, for always being encouraging and uplifting and for making it feel like it could actually be possible. You are truly one of the most talented people I know and I feel incredibly privileged to have worked with you on this.

Thank you to Ola Smit, whose photography transports me to wherever she is in that captured moment. I have admired your work for so long and it was a total dream to work with you. In fact it was pure delight! I feel I have made a friend for life and I will treasure the images forever. Thank you to Emma Cantlay, Katie Smith, Liv Georgiadis, Martyna Wlodarska and Yolaine Campana for helping to ensure that the shoot ran deliciously and smoothly, and thank you to Oli Kember for bringing excellent vibes. They say it takes a village and I am so grateful that for those two weeks you were my village.

Thank you to Kait Polkinghorne for making this book the lovely looking thing that she is now. Thank you for being so patient and accommodating with all the tweaks and colour adjustments, no matter how big or small they were. I love seeing this book on my shelf.

To my wonderful mad family. I love you. Thank you to my siblings, Natasha, William and Camilla. I love feeding you all. I love that you let me do the cooking and I love even more that you do the washing up. I can't wait for you to cook from the pages of this book. Thank you to my parents for always supporting me. Thank you to Mama for always welcoming me home with a stack full of magazine pages of recipes or pictures you thought I might find inspiring. Thank you for teaching me how to host and most importantly how to have fun whilst doing so. It makes me so happy that you have cooked so many of these recipes already. I am so glad that they are now all in one place. Daddy, I don't need to tell you this, but you are my rock. Thank you for always picking up the phone and for listening. Thank you for helping me to see that there is always a solution to any problem and for teaching me to find it. Thank you for your enthusiasm in trying all my recipes (the successes and 'could be betters')

and for being excited about each and every one, even though you'd be very happy with a bowl of cereal. Thank you to my extended family, to Spencer and Dani, Christopher and Jane, Chris and Emma, Ben, and Nikki. Thank you for all the continued support over the years. To dear Linda, my fairy godmother. You have always made me feel like I could do anything. So many of my fondest memories are sitting with you watching Nigella on TV and trawling through the Christmas food magazines over a stir-fry. I hope this book makes you proud.

To Freddie, my best friend and my whole heart. I simply could not have done any of it without you. Thank you for putting up with me, through all the tears and doubts. Thank you for the late-night butter and sugar runs when I was round eight of cake testing but thought I just needed to test it one more time. Thank you for so often giving up your weekends to help me work and for always listening to my constant chatter about what I plan on cooking. Thank you for teaching me so much of what I know when it comes to anything photography or film related. You are a very sexy teacher. Thank you for being the best Papa ever to our little girl and for dancing this freelance juggle with both determination and joy. We are so lucky!

Thank you to my baby girl, Anabel. You amaze me every day. I am so thrilled that you have such a curious and eager appetite. I feel so proud to be your Mama. You make me happier than you know.

X

INDEX

Note: page numbers in **bold** refer to illustrations.

A

agrodolce aubergines 51
aioli 194
ajo blanco and spring onion with charred lettuce 138, **139**
almond
    apricot, ricotta and almond cake 170, **171**
    baked chicken with La Ratte potatoes and romesco **110**, 111
    charred lettuce, with ajo blanco and spring onion 138, **139**
    frangipane 164–5, **165**, **174**, 175
    fruit and nut rice 87, **120–1**
    olive salsa 64, **65**
    roasted cherry almond tart 164–5, **165**
    winter greens with almonds and figs **36**, 37
almond liqueur
    apricot, ricotta and almond cake 170, **171**
    no-churn raspberry ripple ice cream 167
amaretti and whipped honey yogurt with baked figs and plums 172, **173**
anchovy
    cavolo nero with anchovy, chilli and hazelnuts 63
    courgette, anchovy and lemon fritti **56**, 57
    hake puttanesca 105, **107**
    new potatoes with anchovy chive butter **76**, 77
    queen Caesar salad **22**, 23
    salsa verde 25, 196
    tomato salad 41
    winter greens with almonds and figs **36**, 37
apple
    cider-braised chicken with apples **126**, 127
    za'atar cabbage, fennel, apple slaw 40
apricot, ricotta and almond cake 170, **171**
artichoke
    artichoke, fennel and Parmesan salad 16, **17**
    charred artichokes on minty yogurt **46**, 47
asparagus
    asparagus and green bean mimosa salad **14**, 15
    springtime fritters **48**, 49–50
aubergine
    agrodolce aubergines 51
    grilled aubergines with green tahini 134, **135**
    spiced aubergine on cold garlic yogurt **70**, 71

B

balance 9
basil
    chicken with saffron and chickpeas 104
    green beans with Pecorino and pine nuts 34, **35**
    one-tray spatchcocked chicken with herby rice 114, **115**
    salsa verde 196
    sticky lemony courgette rice 74, **75**
batter mixes **48**, 49–50, **56**, 57
bean(s)
    asparagus and green bean mimosa salad **14**, 15
    brothy beans with cavolo nero and chicken **88**, 89
    green beans with Pecorino and pine nuts 34, **35**
    saffron butter beans **84**, 85
beef, herby meatballs with green tahini 60, **61**
beetroot roasted with whipped feta and green chilli salsa 116, **117**
bitter leaf salad with soft eggs 38, **39**
black treacle, spiced ginger cake with whipped mascarpone **180**, 181
bread
    no-knead spelt loaf 204
    soda bread 200, **201**
    wholegrain flatbreads **198**, 199
    wholegrain focaccia 202–3, **203**
breadcrumbs **22**, 23
bream grilled with charred spring onion salsa 147, **148–9**
brothy beans with cavolo nero and chicken **88**, 89
brownie, molten chocolate skillet 179
burrata
    charred spring onions with burrata, peas and dill **142**, 143
    fennel, shallot, tomato and garlic confit with burrata 108, **109**
    nectarines with burrata and pink peppercorns 20, **21**
butter
    anchovy chive **76**, 77
    caper lemon garlic 205
    compound 205
    garlic herb **198**, 199
    hazelnut chilli 118
    honey lime 140, **141**
    pistachio chilli herb 54, **55**
    rosemary chilli and walnut 205
    sage pecan 82–3, **83**

sesame honey miso 205
butter bean
   brothy beans with cavolo nero
      and chicken **88**, 89
   saffron butter beans **84**, 85

C

cabbage
   grilled cabbage with honey lime
      butter 140, **141**
   za'atar cabbage, fennel, apple slaw 40
Caesar salad, queen **22**, 23
cakes
   apricot, ricotta and almond cake 170, **171**
   flourless chocolate meringue
      cake 158, **159**
   spiced ginger cake with whipped
      mascarpone **180**, 181
Campari and blood orange jelly 178
cannellini bean, brothy beans with cavolo
   nero and chicken **88**, 89
caper(s)
   agrodolce aubergines 51
   artichoke, fennel and Parmesan
      salad 16, **17**
   asparagus and green bean mimosa
      salad **14**, 15
   baked ricotta with Romano
      peppers 102, **103**
   caper, lemon and garlic butter 205
   hake puttanesca 105, **107**
   loaded feta with peach, olives
      and herbs 28, **29**
   olive salsa 64, **65**
   salsa verde 25, 196
   tomato salad 41
caramel, no-churn miso caramel pecan
   ice cream 166, **168–9**
carrot
   carrot and coriander salad 24
   cider-braised chicken with apples **126**, 127
   harissa sesame carrots with labneh **94**, 95
   red wine-braised lentil(s) 86
cavolo nero
   brothy beans with cavolo nero
      and chicken **88**, 89
   cavolo nero with anchovy, chilli
      and hazelnuts 63
   cider-braised chicken with apples **126**, 127
   red wine-braised lentil(s) 86
   winter greens with almonds
      and figs **36**, 37
cheese *see* burrata; feta; mozzarella;
   Parmesan; Pecorino; ricotta

cherry, roasted cherry almond
   tart 164–5, **165**
chicken
   baked chicken with La Ratte potatoes
      and romesco **110**, 111
   brothy beans with cavolo nero
      and chicken **88**, 89
   chicken with saffron and chickpeas 104
   cider-braised chicken with apples **126**, 127
   crispy chicken thighs with lemon
      and pink peppercorns 119
   harissa honey chicken wings 150, **151**
   one-tray spatchcocked chicken with
      herby rice 114, **115**
   pan-fried chicken with chilli, tomatoes
      and mint **26–7**, 58, **59**
chickpea(s)
   chicken with saffron and chickpeas 104
   soft courgettes with chickpeas, lemon
      and mint 78, **79**
chicory and pear seeded salad 32, **33**
chilli
   baked salmon with blood orange
      and chilli 122, **123**
   cavolo nero with anchovy, chilli
      and hazelnuts 63
   green chilli salsa 116, **117**
   hazelnut chilli butter 118
   pan-fried chicken with chilli, tomatoes
      and mint **26–7**, 58, **59**
   pickled chilli salsa **136**, 137
   pistachio chilli herb butter 54, **55**
   rosemary, chilli and walnut butter 205
chive(s)
   new potatoes with anchovy chive
      butter **76**, 77
   pea, pancetta and Pecorino tart 100–1
   smoky chipotle prawn cocktail 30, **31**
chocolate
   chocolate marmalade tart 176, **177**
   flourless chocolate meringue
      cake 158, **159**
   molten chocolate skillet brownie 179
cider-braised chicken with apples **126**, 127
coffee liqueur, pistachio
   tiramisu **160**, 161, **162–3**
confit garlic 197
coriander (fresh)
   carrot and coriander salad 24
   charred spring onion salsa 147, **148–9**
coriander seed
   carrot and coriander salad 24
   loaded feta with peach, olives
      and herbs 28, **29**

courgette
   courgette, anchovy and lemon fritti **56**, 57
   pan-fried courgettes with mozzarella
      and pistachio butter 54, **55**
   soft courgettes with chickpeas, lemon
      and mint 78, **79**
   sticky lemony courgette rice 74, **75**
crab, prawn and tomato spaghetti **72**, 73
crackers, seeded spelt 206, **207**
cream
   chocolate marmalade tart 176, **177**
   no-churn miso caramel pecan
      ice cream 166, **168–9**
   no-churn raspberry ripple ice
      cream 167
   pea, pancetta and Pecorino tart 100–1
   whipped honey yogurt cream 172, **173**
   whipped mascarpone frosting **180**, 181
crème fraîche, fennel and thyme
   gratin 124, **125**

D

date(s) (Medjool), spiced aubergine
   on cold garlic yogurt **70**, 71
dill
   charred spring onions with burrata,
      peas and dill **142**, 143
   fruit and nut rice 87, **120–1**
   herb salad with crushed
      hazelnuts 18, **19**, **120–1**
   herby meatballs with green tahini 60, **61**
   one-tray spatchcocked chicken with
      herby rice 114, **115**
   pea, pancetta and Pecorino tart 100–1
   za'atar cabbage, fennel, apple slaw 40
dressings **14**, 15, 18, **19**, 20, **21**, 30, **31**, 32,
   33, **36**, 37–8, **39**, 40–1
   ajo blanco 138, **139**
   queen Caesar salad **22**, 23
   sesame miso 189
   tahini 187

E

egg
- apricot, ricotta and almond cake 170, **171**
- asparagus and green bean mimosa salad **14**, 15
- bitter leaf salad with soft eggs 38, **39**
- flourless chocolate meringue cake 158, **159**
- frangipane 164–5, **165**
- mayonnaise 194–5
- molten chocolate skillet brownie 179
- no-churn miso caramel pecan ice cream 166, **168–9**
- pea, pancetta and Pecorino tart 100–1
- pistachio tiramisu 160, 161, **162–3**
- potato rösti with fried eggs and soft herbs 62
- savoury shortcrust pastry 208
- spiced ginger cake with whipped mascarpone **180**, 181
- sweet shortcrust pastry 209

entertaining 9

F

fennel
- artichoke, fennel and Parmesan salad 16, **17**
- brothy beans with cavolo nero and chicken **88**, 89
- cider-braised chicken with apples **126**, 127
- crispy chicken thighs with lemon and pink peppercorns 119
- fennel, thyme and crème fraîche gratin 124, **125**
- hake puttanesca 105, **107**
- one-tray spatchcocked chicken with herby rice 114, **115**
- red wine-braised lentil(s) 86
- shallot, tomato and garlic confit with burrata 108, **109**
- za'atar cabbage, fennel, apple slaw 40

fennel seed vinaigrette 186

feta
- charred lettuce on whipped feta with pickled chilli salsa **136**, 137
- filo baked feta with harissa and honey 98, **99**
- loaded feta with peach, olives and herbs 28, **29**
- prawn saganaki 52, **53**
- roasted beetroot with whipped feta and green chilli salsa 116, **117**
- stuffed squid with tomatoes and feta 144–5, **145**
- whipped feta 192

fig
- baked figs and plums with whipped honey yogurt and amaretti 172, **173**
- fig and pecan soda bread 200
- fruit and nut rice 87, **120–1**
- winter greens with almonds and figs 36, 37

filo baked feta with harissa and honey 98, **99**

fish
- baked salmon with blood orange and chilli 122, **123**
- grilled bream with charred spring onion salsa 147, **148–9**
- hake puttanesca 105, **107**
- pan-fried sea bass with olive salsa 64, **65**
- *see also* anchovy

flapjack, strawberry flapjack tart **156**, 157

flatbread
- wholegrain flatbreads **198**, 199
- wholegrain focaccia 202–3, **203**

focaccia, wholegrain 202–3, **203**

frangipane
- pear and hazelnut frangipane galette **174**, 175
- roasted cherry almond tart 164–5, **165**

fritters, springtime **48**, 49–50

fritti, courgette, anchovy and lemon 56, **57**

frosting, whipped mascarpone **180**, 181

fruit and nut rice 87, **120–1**

G

galette, pear and hazelnut frangipane **174**, 175

garlic
- caper lemon garlic butter 205
- confit garlic 197
- fennel, shallot, tomato and garlic confit with burrata 108, **109**
- garlic herb butter **198**, 199
- garlic yogurt **70**, 71
- roasted garlic yogurt **96**, 97

ginger, spiced ginger cake with whipped mascarpone **180**, 181

gnudi with roasted tomato sauce 112–13, **113**

golden syrup, spiced ginger cake with whipped mascarpone **180**, 181

Grana Padano
- Grana Padano and rosemary soda bread 200
- *see also* Parmesan

gratin, fennel, thyme and crème fraîche 124, **125**

Greek yogurt
- garlic yogurt **70**, 71
- labneh 190, **191**
- queen Caesar salad dressing **22**, 23
- roasted garlic yogurt **96**, 97
- whipped feta 192
- whipped honey yogurt cream 172, **173**
- whipped tahini yogurt 193

green bean
- asparagus and green bean mimosa salad **14**, 15
- green beans with Pecorino and pine nuts 34, **35**

green chilli salsa 116, **117**

green tahini 188
- grilled aubergines with green tahini 134, **135**
- herby meatballs with green tahini 60, **61**

H

hake puttanesca 105, **107**

harissa
- filo baked feta with harissa and honey 98, **99**
- harissa honey chicken wings 150, **151**
- harissa sesame carrots with labneh **94**, 95

hazelnut
- cavolo nero with anchovy, chilli and hazelnuts 63
- fruit and nut rice 87, **120–1**
- hazelnut chilli butter 118
- herb salad with crushed hazelnuts 18, **19**, **120–1**
- pear and hazelnut frangipane galette **174**, 175

herb(s)
- garlic herb butter **198**, 199
- herb salad with crushed hazelnuts 18, **19**, **120–1**
- herby meatballs with green tahini 60, **61**
- herby rice 114, **115**
- loaded feta with peach, olives and herbs 28, **29**
- pistachio chilli herb butter 54, **55**
- potato rösti with fried eggs and soft herbs 62
- *see also specific herbs*

honey
- filo baked feta with harissa and honey 98, **99**
- harissa honey chicken wings 150, **151**

honey lime butter 140, **141**
honeyed tahini **94**, 95
sesame, honey and miso butter 205
whipped honey yogurt cream 172, **173**

I

ice cream
   no-churn miso caramel pecan 166, **168–9**
   no-churn raspberry ripple 167

J

jelly, Campari and blood orange 178

K

kale, red wine-braised lentil(s) 86

L

labneh 190, **191**
   harissa sesame carrots with labneh **94**, 95
lamb, butterflied leg of lamb with red wine vinegar 146
leek baked with hazelnut chilli butter 118
lemon
   caper lemon garlic butter 205
   charred spring onions with burrata, peas and dill **142**, 143
   courgette, anchovy and lemon fritti **56**, 57
   crab, prawn and tomato spaghetti **72**, 73
   crispy chicken thighs with lemon and pink peppercorns 119
   fruit and nut rice 87, **120–1**
   gnudi with roasted tomato sauce 112–13, **113**
   green tahini 188
   grilled bream with charred spring onion salsa 147, **148–9**
   grilled sugar snap peas with lemony ricotta **132**, 133
   one-tray spatchcocked chicken with herby rice 114, **115**
   pappardelle with walnuts, nutmeg and lemon 80, **81**
   pickled chilli salsa **136**, 137
   soft courgettes with chickpeas, lemon and mint 78, **79**
   springtime fritters **48**, 49–50
   sticky lemony courgette rice 74, **75**
   strawberry flapjack tart **156**, 157
   whipped feta 192
   whipped tahini yogurt 193

lentil(s), red wine-braised 86
lettuce (baby gem)
   charred lettuce with ajo blanco and spring onion 138, **139**
   charred lettuce on whipped feta with pickled chilli salsa **136**, 137
   salsa verde salad 25
   smoky chipotle prawn cocktail 30, **31**
lettuce (butterhead), queen Caesar salad **22**, 23
lime
   green chilli salsa 116, **117**
   honey lime butter 140, **141**

M

marinades **26–7**, 58, **59**, 146
marmalade chocolate tart 176, **177**
mascarpone
   pistachio tiramisu **160**, 161, **162–3**
   whipped mascarpone frosting **180**, 181
mayonnaise 194–5
   aioli 194
   classic 194
   saffron 195
meal planning 8
meatballs, herby meatballs with green tahini 60, **61**
menus 210–13
   A celebration in spring 210
   A slow Sunday (lunch) 210
   An easy Saturday 211
   Just the two of you 213
   Something quick and easy on the sofa 211
   The last-minute dinner party 212
   When the sun is shining 212
   When you want to celebrate 213
meringue cake, flourless chocolate 158, **159**
mint
   fruit and nut rice 87, **120–1**
   green tahini 188
   herb salad with crushed hazelnuts 18, **19**, **120–1**
   herby meatballs with green tahini 60, **61**
   loaded feta with peach, olives and herbs 28, **29**
   minty yogurt **46**, 47
   olive salsa 64, **65**
   one-tray spatchcocked chicken with herby rice 114, **115**
   pan-fried chicken with chilli, tomatoes and mint **26–7**, 58, **59**
   pistachio chilli herb butter 54, **55**

roasted beetroot with whipped feta and green chilli salsa 116, **117**
salsa verde 25, 196
soft courgettes with chickpeas, lemon and mint 78, **79**
miso
   no-churn miso caramel pecan ice cream 166, **168–9**
   sesame, honey and miso butter 205
   sesame miso dressing 189
mozzarella and pistachio butter with pan-fried courgettes 54, **55**

N

nectarines with burrata and pink peppercorns 20, **21**
nut(s)
   fruit and nut rice 87, **120–1**
   see also specific nuts

O

oat(s)
   soda bread 200, **201**
   strawberry flapjack tart **156**, 157
olive(s)
   hake puttanesca 105, **107**
   loaded feta with peach, olives and herbs 28, **29**
   olive salsa 64, **65**
onion squash risotto with sage and pecan butter 82–3, **83**
orange
   baked salmon with blood orange and chilli 122, **123**
   Campari and blood orange jelly 178
   fruit and nut rice 87, **120–1**
orange liqueur, no-churn miso caramel pecan ice cream 166, **168–9**

P

pancetta
  cider-braised chicken with apples **126**, 127
  pea, pancetta and Pecorino tart **100–1**
pappardelle with walnuts, nutmeg and lemon 80, **81**
Parmesan (or Grana Padano)
  artichoke, fennel and Parmesan salad 16, **17**
  chicory and pear seeded salad 32, **33**
  fennel, thyme and crème fraîche gratin 124, **125**
  gnudi with roasted tomato sauce 112–13, **113**
  pappardelle with walnuts, nutmeg and lemon 80, **81**
  queen Caesar salad **22**, 23
  saffron butter beans **84**, 85
  soft courgettes with chickpeas, lemon and mint 78, **79**
  squash risotto with sage and pecan butter 82–3, **83**
  winter greens with almonds and figs **36**, 37
parsley
  agrodolce aubergines 51
  baked ricotta with Romano peppers 102, **103**
  bitter leaf salad with soft eggs 38, **39**
  charred spring onion salsa 147, **148–9**
  fruit and nut rice 87, **120–1**
  green tahini 188
  hake puttanesca 105, **107**
  herb salad with crushed hazelnuts 18, **19**, **120–1**
  herby meatballs with green tahini 60, **61**
  loaded feta with peach, olives and herbs 28, **29**
  olive salsa 64, **65**
  one-tray spatchcocked chicken with herby rice 114, **115**
  pickled chilli salsa **136**, 137
  pistachio chilli herb butter 54, **55**
  roasted beetroot with whipped feta and green chilli salsa 116, **117**
  salsa verde 25, 196
  tomato salad 41
  za'atar cabbage, fennel, apple slaw 40
pasta
  crab, prawn and tomato spaghetti **72**, 73
  pappardelle with walnuts, nutmeg and lemon 80, **81**

pastry
  filo baked feta with harissa and honey 98, **99**
  pea, pancetta and Pecorino tart **100–1**
  savoury shortcrust pastry 208
  see also sweet shortcrust pastry
peach, loaded feta with peach, olives and herbs 28, **29**
pear
  chicory and pear seeded salad 32, **33**
  pear and hazelnut frangipane galette **174**, 175
pea(s)
  charred spring onions with burrata, peas and dill **142**, 143
  pea, pancetta and Pecorino tart **100–1**
pecan nut
  fig and pecan soda bread 200
  no-churn miso caramel pecan ice cream 166, **168–9**
  sage and pecan butter 82–3, **83**
Pecorino
  green beans with Pecorino and pine nuts 34, **35**
  pea, pancetta and Pecorino tart **100–1**
pepper
  baked chicken with La Ratte potatoes and romesco **110**, 111
  baked ricotta with Romano peppers 102, **103**
peppercorn(s)
  crispy chicken thighs with lemon and pink peppercorns 119
  nectarines with burrata and pink peppercorns 20, **21**
pine nut(s)
  asparagus and green bean mimosa salad **14**, 15
  green beans with Pecorino and pine nuts 34, **35**
  sticky lemony courgette rice 74, **75**
pistachio
  fruit and nut rice 87, **120–1**
  pistachio chilli herb butter 54, **55**
  pistachio tiramisu **160**, 161, **162–3**
plating up 9
plum, baked figs and plums with whipped honey yogurt and amaretti 172, **173**
potato
  baked chicken with La Ratte potatoes and romesco **110**, 111
  crispy za'atar-smashed potatoes 96, **97**
  new potatoes with anchovy chive butter **76**, 77
  potato rösti with fried eggs and soft herbs 62

prawn
  crab, prawn and tomato spaghetti **72**, 73
  prawn saganaki 52, **53**
  prawn stock 52, **53**
  smoky chipotle prawn cocktail 30, **31**
puttanesca, hake 105, **107**

Q

queen Caesar salad **22**, 23

R

radicchio (or red chicory), bitter leaf salad with soft eggs 38, **39**
raspberry ripple no-churn ice cream 167
red pepper (roasted), baked chicken with La Ratte potatoes and romesco **110**, 111
red wine-braised lentil(s) 86
rice
  fruit and nut rice 87, **120–1**
  herby rice 114, **115**
  squash risotto with sage and pecan butter 82–3, **83**
  sticky lemony courgette rice 74, **75**
ricotta
  apricot, ricotta and almond cake 170, **171**
  baked ricotta with Romano peppers 102, **103**
  gnudi with roasted tomato sauce 112–13, **113**
  grilled sugar snap peas with lemony ricotta **132**, 133
  strawberry flapjack tart **156**, 157
risotto, squash risotto with sage and pecan butter 82–3, **83**
rocket
  herb salad with crushed hazelnuts 18, **19**, **120–1**
  loaded feta with peach, olives and herbs 28, **29**
Romano pepper with baked ricotta 102, **103**
romesco and La Ratte potatoes with baked chicken **110**, 111
rosemary
  grana padano and rosemary soda bread 200
  rosemary, chilli and walnut butter 205
  wholegrain focaccia 202–3, **203**

S

saffron
  chicken with saffron and chickpeas 104
  saffron butter beans **84**, 85
  saffron mayonnaise 195
saganaki, prawn 52, **53**
sage
  crispy chicken thighs with lemon and pink peppercorns 119
  sage and pecan butter 82–3, **83**
salads 10–41
  artichoke, fennel and Parmesan salad 16, **17**
  asparagus and green bean mimosa salad **14**, 15
  bitter leaf salad with soft eggs 38, **39**
  carrot and coriander salad 24
  chicory and pear seeded salad 32, **33**
  green beans with Pecorino and pine nuts 34, **35**
  herb salad with crushed hazelnuts 18, **19**, **120–1**
  loaded feta with peach, olives and herbs 28, **29**
  nectarines with burrata and pink peppercorns 20, **21**
  queen Caesar salad **22**, 23
  salsa verde salad 25
  smoky chipotle prawn cocktail 30, **31**
  tomato salad 41
  winter greens with almonds and figs 36, **37**
  za'atar cabbage, fennel, apple slaw 40
salmon baked with blood orange and chilli 122, **123**
salsa
  charred spring onion 147, **148–9**
  green chilli 116, **117**
  olive 64, **65**
  pickled chilli **136**, 137
  tomato **136**, 137
salsa verde
  salsa verde salad 25
  salsa verde two ways 196
sauce, roasted tomato 112–13, **113**
savoiardi (ladyfinger) biscuits, pistachio tiramisu **160**, 161, **162–3**
sea bass
  grilled sea bass with charred spring onion salsa 147, **148–9**
  pan-fried sea bass with olive salsa 64, **65**
seeded spelt crackers 206, **207**
sesame oil
  sesame, honey and miso butter 205

sesame miso dressing 189
sesame seed(s)
  grilled cabbage with honey lime butter 140, **141**
  harissa sesame carrots with labneh **94**, 95
  seeded spelt crackers 206, **207**
  sesame, honey and miso butter 205
shallot, fennel, tomato and garlic confit with burrata 108, **109**
shortcrust pastry
  savoury 208
  see also sweet shortcrust pastry
slaw, za'atar cabbage, fennel, apple 40
soda bread 200, **201**
  fig and pecan 200
  Grana Padano and rosemary 200
space issues 8
spelt flour
  apricot, ricotta and almond cake 170, **171**
  chocolate marmalade tart 176, **177**
  no-knead spelt loaf 204
  pea, pancetta and Pecorino tart 100–1
  savoury shortcrust pastry 208
  seeded spelt crackers 206, **207**
  soda bread 200, **201**
  strawberry flapjack tart **156**, 157
  sweet shortcrust pastry 209
  wholegrain flatbreads **198**, 199
spinach, gnudi with roasted tomato sauce 112–13, **113**
spring onion
  charred lettuce with ajo blanco and spring onion 138, **139**
  charred spring onion salsa 147, **148–9**
  charred spring onions with burrata, peas and dill **142**, 143
  fruit and nut rice 87, **120–1**
  springtime fritters **48**, 49–50
  sticky lemony courgette rice 74, **75**
springtime fritters **48**, 49–50
squash risotto with sage and pecan butter 82–3, **83**
squid stuffed with tomatoes and feta 144–5, **145**
stock, prawn 52, **53**
strawberry flapjack tart **156**, 157
sugar snap pea(s) grilled with lemony ricotta **132**, 133
sun-blushed tomato, agrodolce aubergines 51
sunflower seed
  carrot and coriander salad 24
  chicory and pear seeded salad 32, **33**
  za'atar cabbage, fennel, apple slaw 40

sweet shortcrust pastry 209
  chocolate marmalade tart 176, **177**
  pear and hazelnut frangipane galette **174**, 175
  roasted cherry almond tart 164–5, **165**

T

tahini
  green tahini 188
  grilled aubergines with green tahini 134, **135**
  herby meatballs with green tahini 60, **61**
  honeyed tahini **94**, 95
  tahini dressing 187
  whipped tahini yogurt 193
tarragon
  asparagus and green bean mimosa salad **14**, 15
  crab, prawn and tomato spaghetti **72**, 73
  gnudi with roasted tomato sauce 112–13, **113**
  herb salad with crushed hazelnuts 18, **19**, **120–1**
  pea, pancetta and Pecorino tart 100–1
  prawn saganaki 52, **53**
  salsa verde 25, 196
tarts
  chocolate marmalade 176, **177**
  pea, pancetta and Pecorino 100–1
  roasted cherry almond 164–5, **165**
  strawberry flapjack **156**, 157
  Tenderstem broccoli, springtime fritters **48**, 49–50
thyme, crème fraîche and fennel gratin 124, **125**
time constraints 8
tiramisu, pistachio **160**, 161, **162–3**
tomato
  agrodolce aubergines 51
  crab, prawn and tomato spaghetti **72**, 73
  fennel, shallot, tomato and garlic confit with burrata 108, **109**
  hake puttanesca 105, **107**
  pan-fried chicken with chilli, tomatoes and mint 26–7, 58, **59**
  prawn saganaki 52, **53**
  roasted tomato sauce 112–13, **113**
  spiced aubergine on cold garlic yogurt **70**, 71
  stuffed squid with tomatoes and feta 144–5, **145**
  tomato salad 41
  tomato salsa **136**, 137

221

V

vinaigrette, fennel seed 186

W

walnut
  pappardelle with walnuts, nutmeg and lemon 80, **81**
  rosemary, chilli and walnut butter 205
white wine
  baked chicken with La Ratte potatoes and romesco **110**, 111
  chicken with saffron and chickpeas 104
  crab, prawn and tomato spaghetti **72**, 73
  crispy chicken thighs with lemon and pink peppercorns 119
  hake puttanesca 105, **107**
  one-tray spatchcocked chicken with herby rice 114, **115**
  squash risotto with sage and pecan butter 82–3, **83**
wholegrain flatbreads **198**, 199
wild garlic, springtime fritters **48**, 49–50
wine
  red wine-braised lentil(s) 86
  see also white wine
winter greens with almonds and figs **36**, 37

Y

yogurt
  minty yogurt **46**, 47
  soda bread 200, **201**
  wholegrain flatbreads **198**, 199
  see also Greek yogurt

Z

za'atar
  crispy za'atar smashed potatoes 96, **97**
  herby meatballs with green tahini 60, **61**
  za'atar cabbage, fennel, apple slaw 40